George Edward Stubbs

Practical Hints on Boy Choir Training

George Edward Stubbs

Practical Hints on Boy Choir Training

ISBN/EAN: 9783337296582

Printed in Europe, USA, Canada, Australia, Japan

Cover: Foto ©Thomas Meinert / pixelio.de

More available books at **www.hansebooks.com**

PRACTICAL HINTS

ON THE

Training of Choir Boys

BY

G. EDWARD STUBBS, M.A., MUS.DOC.

Organist and Choirmaster of St. Agnes' Chapel, Trinity Parish, New York

WITH AN INTRODUCTION BY

THE REV. J. S. B. HODGES, D.D.

Rector of St. Paul's Church, Baltimore, Md.

"The music of the sanctuary must be treated not in a sentimental, but in a very business-like way, like any other enterprise, whether secular or sacred: for no amount of pious intention can dispense with the fullest use of legitimate means to attain the end in view."—THE PARISH GUIDE.

TWELFTH EDITION

THE H. W. GRAY CO.
SOLE AGENTS FOR
NOVELLO & CO., Ltd.
2 WEST 45TH STREET, NEW YORK

To

PREFACE.

THE author of the following pages has frequently been urged by clergymen, and others, interested in vested choirs, to write a manual of choir-training, adapted to the wants of organists and choir-directors, entrusted with the management of boy-choirs. In compliance, it has been his aim not only to give *practical suggestions* regarding choir-work, but also to call special attention to the importance of sound *vocal* training. In this latter task he disclaims any originality in the vocal theories advanced, all of which are supported by standard writers on the voice.

No less an authority than J. Spencer Curwen, Associate of the Royal Academy of Music, England, takes the ground that boys' voices are very seldom properly trained. He thus describes the usual defects in the singing of choristers :

"They cannot sing the soprano part unless it happens to lie low, and when it does they sing harshly, and afford pain rather than pleasure to the listener. If the part lies in the upper half of their compass their voices soon tire ; they waver like the nearly exhausted pipe of an organ, they flatten atrociously, and they wear out long before the natural change to the man's voice. If the melody leaps to F or G (at the top of the treble staff) they become inaudible, and when a high note of

this sort follows the C or A below, which has probably
been delivered with piercing force, the contrast would
be comic if it were not so very disagreeable. Properly
trained boys, on the contrary, have a wide and even
compass."

Clergymen often express surprise that some of the
most important principles of voice culture are neglected in choir-training—a fact abundantly proved by the
prevailing paucity of really fine boy-choirs. Choir-
masters, in seeking information regarding boys' voices,
look for *special hints,* and are often compelled to wade
through a long list of books, without finding anything
that will *directly* help them in their work. The knowledge sought for is spread over too wide a field of reading to be readily available. This fact has undoubtedly
acted as a drawback to many desirous of extending
their views on the subject. Of the numerous excellent books * on choir-training which have been published from time to time, it is singular that few refer
with sufficient *clearness* to the difficulties met with in
the training of boys' voices. Whether the authors of
these various works have considered it unwise to give
any *detailed* plan of vocal procedure, or whether they
have deemed it unnecessary, does not appear. The
fact remains that there are scarcely any manuals of
choir-training at present which meet the wants of the
fast-increasing number of choir-masters who stand in
need of vocal knowledge.

The art of boy choir-training is, strictly speaking, in
its infancy here in the United States.† Vested choirs,

* They are almost exclusively English works.

† Even in England, the growth of vested choirs outside of the
cathedrals is comparatively recent. Frederick Helmore wrote in 1878,

notwithstanding their rapid growth, are still in the minority. The professional organist and choir-master generally finds himself called upon to train men and women. This affords him little if any practice even in *general* voice culture, much less in its special branches. The voices of men and women, even though untrained, are comparatively pure and musical as regards *timbre*, and are immediately available for choral purposes. Vocal culture, *per se*, however desirable, is not in their case necessary. The director of such a body of singers chiefly trains them to sing together, in time, and with proper expression. There his work ends.

The case is vastly different with the vocal trainer of boys. The average boy voice, in its *natural*, untrained state, is musically disagreeable, and must undergo a radical modification before it can be utilized for musical purposes.

The author believes this fact to be overlooked by many clergymen who introduce boy-choirs into their parishes. He knows that choir-masters accustomed to train "quartette" and chorus choirs, upon being called upon to train boy-choristers, are more or less baffled by the vocal difficulties inevitably encountered in the work.*

It is a matter of regret that more has not been especially written about the boy voice, as there is room for additional light on the subject.

" Forty years ago, with very few exceptions, there were no surpliced choirs, except in cathedrals and collegiate chapels. The singers were mostly placed in a gallery at the western end of the church. . . . The treble was principally sustained by female voices."

* An emergency of no rare occurrence in these days.

In issuing this little work, the author feels that, whatever may be its outcome in the way of criticism, it is
at all events a step in the right direction.   If it clears
away any of the obstacles usually met with in fitting
boys for their duties as choristers, he will believe that
he has served well the cause of Church music.

G. E. S.

Sᴛ. Jᴀᴍᴇs' Cʜᴜʀᴄʜ, Nᴇᴡ Yᴏʀᴋ, October, 1888.

PREFACE TO THE SIXTH EDITION.

Tʜᴀᴛ five editions of this manual have been exhausted within a comparatively short time, is a hopeful
indication that it is fulfilling its mission as a practical
guide to the choirmaster's art.

It may also be looked upon as an encouraging sign,
that the introduction of vested choirs of boys and men,
in the American branch of the Church, is becoming, if
not universal, nearly so.

There is an unmistakable tendency to return to
churchly usages, *musically* as well as otherwise.   But
aside from this, viewed from a *scientific* standpoint, the
progress made by our choirs in recent years is most
marked.   Absolute purity of tone, that all-important
factor in the rendition of the choral service, has been,
until quite lately, a secondary matter ; now it is becoming an important test of the choirmaster's skill.

The author feels thankful that this book has helped
to raise the standard of choir-training in this country,
and that it has been so favorably received in England,
the home of the great cathedral choirs.

Sᴛ. Aɢɴᴇs' Cʜᴀᴘᴇʟ, Tʀɪɴɪᴛʏ Pᴀʀɪsʜ, Nᴇᴡ Yᴏʀᴋ,
April, 1892.

PREFACE TO THE REVISED EDITION.

THE changes in this edition consist chiefly in the addition of a new chapter (in the form of an Appendix) and an alteration in the title, from "Practical Hints on Boy Choir Training" to "Practical Hints on the Training of Choir Boys."

English readers are reminded that the expression "Boy Choir" is a colloquialism in the American branch of the Church. It came into use about thirty years ago, when male choirs began to displace "quartettes," as they were called, *i.e.*, choirs consisting of four singers, a bass, a tenor, a woman contralto, and a woman soprano. ("Quartette" in this particular sense is also an Americanism.)

By way of distinction, choirs of men and boys were called "Boy Choirs." Strictly speaking, the term is an incorrect one, and although it occurs occasionally in this book, it appears no longer on the title page.

The author desires to return his sincere thanks to the firm of Novello, Ewer & Co., for the many courtesies shown him, and for the liberal spirit in which they have introduced this work into musical circles in England.

ST. AGNES' CHAPEL, TRINITY PARISH, NEW YORK.
January, 1897.

LIST OF WORKS REFERRED TO.

A.—A Dictionary of Music and Musicians. Edited by George Grove, D.C.L.

B.—Voice, Song, and Speech. By Browne and Behnke.

C.—The Voice in Singing. By Madame Seiler.

D.—Advice to Singers by a Singer.

E.—The Mechanism of the Human Voice. By Emil Behnke.

F.—The Child's Voice. By Browne and Behnke.

G.—Studies in Worship Music. By J. Spencer Curwen.

H.—The Art of Singing. By A. B. Bach.

The Art of Training Choir Boys. By Dr. G. C. Martin.

The Boy's Voice. By J. Spencer Curwen.

Organ Accompaniment. By J. F. Bridge.

Reference is made by giving the respective letter prefixed to each work, and the number of page.

CONTENTS.

"I have found it an art by itself to teach children singing. It requires the *most careful gentle treatment,* much more so than the cultivation of the voices of adults demands; and therefore only the best teachers should be trusted with the cultivation of children's voices."—MADAME EMMA SEILER.

INTRODUCTION.

THE rapid increase in the number of what are called
" Boy-choirs " is one of the signs of the times—a good
sign ; but it is also one attended with many practical
difficulties, and the Church will owe a debt of gratitude to anyone who can give such " practical hints "
as may tend to remove or lessen these difficulties.

The changes which have been made in the composition, and in the position, of the choir, are very marked.
It is only a short time since, with the exception of the
Cathedrals and Collegiate Churches in England, the
choirs of our churches, in England and in this country,
were composed of men and women singers, placed
aloft in a gallery, generally at the western end of the
church, entirely separated from the congregation, and
shut in by curtains which excluded them from all
observation.

By this isolated position, as well as oftentimes by the
character of the music sung, these singers monopolized
entirely this portion of the service, and that in a way
not always inspiring devotion, or tending to edification.

Perhaps this state of things had more to do than is
generally supposed, with the separation of the Meth-
odists from the Church of England. That separation
was not made on doctrinal grounds ; it did not arise
from differing teaching on Baptism, Eucharist, or

Episcopacy. It was due more to the coldness and inanition of the Church, the lack of warm and living services ; and if, instead of having to listen to the praises of God sung for them by those who too often had no thought of praising God in their hearts, they had had the opportunity of taking their own part in singing such hymns as are now to be found throughout the Church, it may be that that great schism would never have occurred, or at least that thousands would have been saved from it.

Be this as it may, very great are the changes since those days. Choirs and organs have been brought down from their elevation, and placed nearer the people. The people have in measure learned their duty, and accepted the privilege of taking part in their portion of Divine worship. Hymns new and old have been sanctioned and brought into use, bringing in with them a flood of music, which has spread its waves throughout the Church ; and in thousands of congregations to-day there is a life, and a fervor, and a spirit utterly unknown half a century ago.

This is only a part of the general revival of Church life, but it is no insignificant part which has been played, whether as a cause or as an instrument of this revival, by the Music of the Church.

In addition to this change of position, there has been the still greater change in the composition of the choirs, effected by the introduction of boys' voices. From Reformation times, probably, boys had been in use in the choirs of Cathedrals and College Chapels ; and they had sung with a clearness, a force, a pathos, which had again and again moved to tears natures not over-susceptible, and called forth expressions of delight from those whose praise was of real value. In these choirs this was, of course, the result of long-continued, careful training. Such excellence is not attained in a day; perhaps hardly in a generation. But here was the evidence of what could be done with this material; and the fact that vast quantities of this material were lying about unused, taken in connection with the universally experienced difficulty of keeping together in harmony, for even a short time, a volunteer choir of the old character, and the equally great difficulty of securing, by pecuniary compensation, the services of fit persons for this duty; all this was more than enough to suggest, almost enough to compel, the use of boys. But a higher and a better feeling has also been at work. We have been coming back to a recognition of what the Church nearer to apostolic times recognized, that the singers in the church have an important and holy office—that they constitute one of the lower ministries, almost an Order. And following out this line of thought, and to bring home to them the sacredness of their office, and to screen them from temptation to irreverence and unseemly behavior, they are given a distinctive dress, a white garment, which is never to be dishonored by improper act or manner. They are placed in full sight of the congregation, and given a position in a very holy part of the church, in the chancel, and near the altar of God. Thus something of the holiness of their office is brought home to them; temptations to irreverence and forgetfulness are lessened, and something which has the nature of actual worship is rendered to Almighty God. For surely, it is not the adult mind only which can enter into worship, or indeed which is most readily moved to emotions of devotion. It has well been said that "in the average youth the religious emotions are as highly developed as in the average mature soprano. Love of God, faith in His power, regret for wrong doing, are qualities which are frequently very highly developed in children, and which, alas! are often dulled or lost as life advances." The movement in favor of "Boy-choirs" is then one in the right direction, and should be encouraged, first because the boy-choir is, upon the whole, certainly the best adapted for the reverent and devout rendering of the musical portion of the worship of Almighty God; and secondly, because of the influence exerted upon the boys themselves, who have the privilege of belonging to a well-ordered choir.

Upon this last point much might be said, but everyone who will pause to think will recognize its importance.

Two other points, not so obvious, may claim a brief passing notice.

The first is this : That the great want now is *a supply of competent Choir-masters.*

In a choir-master is required something more than a knowledge of music, and a capacity to teach music. Without pretending to enumerate all the requirements, there should be a knowledge of Church music, and of Church style, and particularly of that Church music which is suitable for boys' voices ; and, above all, a patient, painstaking, devout spirit. Gentleness, devotion, professional skill, and sufficiency of learning, are essential for a successful choir-master.

Is there no way in which these can be supplied? Is there no place where they can be trained? If there is none, cannot this want be met? Can we not have a

College of Organists and Choir-masters, giving a Certificate of competency to such as have gone through a regular course of study, and successfully stood the required examinations? "Hints" are very good things, very necessary things, to enable one to overcome difficulties, and we welcome them with gratitude. But well-trained Masters would be infinitely better.

And the second point is this : That when such capable men, and well trained, are found, they should be *well paid.*

We should not have boy-choirs because they are cheap methods of praising God, but the Church should make it worth the while of good men, and true, and able, and accomplished, thus to devote themselves to the service of God in His Temple.

J. S, B. H.

CHAPTER I.

BEFORE taking steps to form a choir of boys, the first point to be considered is sufficiency of material, present and prospective. However obvious this may appear, the hint is hardly an unnecessary one. Choirs are often started without accurate judgment as to supply of material, and instances are not wanting where, after premature organization, unlooked-for difficulties are met with in keeping up the required number of voices. To engage in an endless struggle to keep the choir ranks full, is not a judicious undertaking for either rector or choir-master ; it is well, then, to estimate carefully the probabilities as to voice supply* before commencing choir-work.

NUMBER OF BOYS.

For a large church, from sixteen to twenty-four boys (trebles) are needed. For a small church, from ten to fourteen. This is, however, approximate reckoning, as much depends upon the voices and their management.

SOURCES OF MATERIAL.

Choir-schools founded on the English system do not as yet exist in this country. The sources upon which

---

* The word "supply" here has a significant meaning, when we take into account the inevitable changing of boys' voices, and the neces·sity of being continually on the alert to fill vacancies.

our choirs depend for soprano material are the public
schools, the parish schools, and the Sunday-schools. In
large cities, choir-masters obtain their voices not only
from schools, but from various other sources, and their
choirs are largely made up of singers (both men and
boys) who come from outside the parish, and even the
Church itself.* In small places, especially where de-
nominational prejudices are felt, there is a much nar-
rower field to choose from ; and material, if found at
all, is generally found within parochial limits. Consequently, in such places the parish schools and Sunday-schools are of primary importance as reservoirs
from which to draw.

SELECTION OF BOYS.

Boys are useful as choristers when they are between
the ages of ten and sixteen years. Under ten, although
they may possess good voices, they are too young to
evince sufficient musical and general intelligence to be
of much service. Over sixteen, their voices are on the
verge of mutation. Although the younger boys are not
as valuable as the older ones, it is advisable to keep
up a supply of them. Eventually they become the
leaders, and the choir must be filled at one end while it
empties at the other. Bright, nervous, energetic boys
who are fond of music, make the best choristers. Those
who are naturally indolent or deficient in musical in-
stinct should be habitually avoided, even if they have
superior voices. Boys of steady habits and fixed purposes are especially desirable, because they are not

* Choirs exert a missionary influence which is generally under-esti-
mated.   They are frequently the means of bringing into the Church
both men and boys who otherwise might not become churchmen.

likely to give up their choir duties after the novelty of singing has somewhat abated. Changeable choristers are highly undesirable.

LOSS OF CHORISTERS VS. CONTINUITY OF TRAINING.

As vocal training is a slow process, attaining its ends through gradual stages of development, it is of the highest importance that it be continuous and not interrupted. For example, a boy who enters a choir at the age of ten, and remains until his voice breaks, say at the age of fifteen or sixteen, acquires the accumulated benefit of five or six years of vocal instruction and practice. He becomes more and more useful as a chorister, his voice getting stronger and fuller the longer he remains. But if he leaves, say at the age of twelve, he wastes not only what *he* has learned, but he also, in a certain sense, wastes the time of his *choir-master*, who counts upon reaping the results of the previous two years training, and upon the boy's singing longer The rule is, "Retain all voices until they break," although it is often a difficult rule to carry out, excepting in choir-schools and in choirs supported by liberal appropriations. The chief cause of boys giving up choir-work is the breaking of the voice; but there are numerous other causes * constantly encountered by choir-masters. Choristers often grow discontented, whimsical, and "tired of singing." They fall ill, perhaps, or they change their residences, or drift into occupations which prevent their regular attendance at rehearsals.

* Not infrequently, in the larger cities, boys are "bought up" and induced to leave their choir by choir-masters " of easy conscience," who can afford to make it a financial object for them to change. The practice is dishonest.

YEARLY "PERCENTAGE OF CHANGE."

By this is meant the ratio the number of annual losses bears to the number of boys in the choir. Suppose a choir containing fifteen boys to lose three every year, and to gain the same number. The yearly percentage of change would then be 20. This may be considered a low percentage, and very few choirs can boast of it. It is necessary to lessen the percentage of change as much as possible. Where it is high, vocal growth and development are correspondingly low.

PREPARATORY CLASS.

The advisability of forming, in addition to the regular choir, a class of younger boys, called probationers, depends largely upon circumstances. Theoretically, the idea is an excellent one, and should be adopted when it can be successfully carried out. Such a class is especially desirable where there is a large parish school yielding abundance of material ; where there is daily service at which a choir is wanted ; where there is an able assistant organist and choir-master, who can not only utilize the probationers for daily services, but also develop their voices for the choir proper. Where these conditions do not exist, it will be found that the time and trouble spent upon teaching preparatory boys are not always commensurate with after-results. A new boy, upon entering a choir, speedily "falls into the traces," and learns in a month or so as much as he would in double the time as a probationer. Regular choristers act under a stimulus and *esprit de corps* which probationers do not feel, unless they form a separate and active choir by themselves. To keep up a preparatory class requires a considerable amount of energy and training, which often tells more quickly and yields bet‑ ter results if concentrated upon the choir itself.

PROPORTION OF PARTS.

When circumstances permit, there should be as many men as boys in the choir. For example, to balance eighteen well-trained sopranos, there should be eight basses, six tenors, and four altos, if the alto part be sung by men. But voices differ so much in force and carrying power, that no definite rule can be laid down as to proportion of parts. The best results, however, are obtained only when the choir contains a full number of men.* Care should be taken that the alto and tenor parts be not too prominent.

CHORISTERS' STIPENDS.

Frederick Helmore says, "There are three ways of keeping the members of a choir together : 1. By pay‑ ing them. 2. By keeping up the interest of the prac‑ tisings in such a way as to secure a regular attendance for the love of the work. 3. By binding the members together by a common bond of interest. *Of these the first is the simplest.*" Choir-masters are of one mind on this point. The salaried system is, as Helmore says, the *simplest.* The result in the easier enforcement of discipline alone cannot be over-estimated, and there is no more certain method of securing full and regular attendance at rehearsals and services. It is true that

* Besides the harmonic gain, bold unison passages ring out with telling effect when the choir is plentifully supplied with adult voices. In small choirs, where the boys are supported by a few men, unison music is generally ineffective.

some rectors and choir-masters, by personal influence, succeed in maintaining a complete volunteer chorus; but this is decidedly exceptional. However important the moral effect of such voluntary service may seem, it is not infrequently secured at the loss of other advantages which more than balance the supposed gain.

Nearly all successful * choirs are salaried choirs. There is perhaps no more serious obstacle to a choir-master's work than the want of a sufficient appropriation for choristers' stipends. "If I have a choir, it must not be a *voluntary* one. I will not be subject to the whims and fancies of the singers, or liable to have all the tenors absent, or all the altos. If I have a choir, it must be a *paid* one, whose services I can command." Henry Smart. (G. 167.)

VOLUNTEER MEN.

There are, nevertheless, many parishes of limited means, where the payment of numerous salaries is out of the question. In such places the success of a choir depends upon the personal influence of the rector and the musical abilities of the choir-master. When no salaries are paid, the incentives to choir-work are : 1. Sense of duty in helping on the Church by volunteer performance. 2. Musical interest engendered by the choir-master through his successful training, leading on to a desire to sing from educational motives, and for musical pleasure. However selfish this latter incentive may seem, it is practically the one to which, on the choir-master's part, chief attention must be paid. Such motives, although not the true ones, should be recognized for the sake of what they may ultimately lead to.

* The word here refers to *musical* success in its strict sense.

(See note, p. 20.) The better the choir, the greater will be the number of volunteer singers. It is a good plan, however, always to pay the boys, even if the rest of the choir be not paid. Choir-boys, it should be remembered, are but children, and can comprehend but dimly the idea of singing from a sense of duty. The expense of paying them is comparatively trifling, while the inconveniences resulting from not paying them are often serious. There are exceptions to the rule, of course, and boys who cheerfully offer their services to the Church should be received as volunteers, and commended for their praiseworthy action.

ORGANIST AND CHOIR-MASTER.

The duties of organist and choir-master are sometimes divided and assigned to different officers. As a rule, there is no particular advantage in this. Although it is not always possible to find combined in one individual the qualities which make a successful voice-trainer, choir-master, and organist, it is nevertheless highly desirable that these functions should be vested in one and the same person. At services the organist is practically the conductor of the music. Through his manipulation of the organ he establishes a subtle understanding between himself and his choir, which is of the highest importance, and which, if he alone trains his singers, he uses to far greater advantage than if he acts as a subordinate.

THE CHIEF DIFFICULTIES.

It is not primarily from *musical*, but *ecclesiastical*, reasons that boy-choirs are employed in churches. The influence of Church tradition in this regard is seen in the constantly and rapidly increasing number of vested choirs all over the country. It is undeniable, however, that while male choirs are most desirable from the ecclesiastical point of view, they have musical draw-backs which occasionally discourage their most earnest advocates. The fact that boys lose their voices at the age of sixteen years is of itself a disadvantage, for it involves the incessant replenishing of the choir with young and inexperienced choristers, and the continual loss of the oldest and most valuable ones. The choir-master in his vocal training works, so to speak, "against time." He must patiently labor over the development of voices, knowing full well that before he reaches mature vocal ability on the part of his choristers, nature will step in and defeat him. The second disadvantage is that boys' voices, unlike those of women, sound, in their natural state, coarse and rasping to refined, sensitive ears. It is only after a skilful course of training that they become agreeable, and consequently, only in parishes where expert choir-masters are in command are desirable *vocal results* secured. On the other hand, we should not lose sight of the fact that choirs of men and women likewise have serious drawbacks, and are proverbially hard to manage. The vocal difficulties of boy choir-training although great, are far from insurmountable ; more over, in places where it has been found impossible to maintain a high degree of vocal proficiency among choristers, vested choirs have nevertheless been the means of reviving the interest in Church music, and have incontestably proved their *general* superiority to other forms of choirs.

CHAPTER II.

UNDER this heading, a point of primary importance is the position of the church organ, which (it would seem almost unnecessary to say) should be in the chancel.

In modern church buildings provision is generally made for this. There are, however, numbers of churches where the old gallery organ is left in its original position, after the " quartette " has given place to a vested choir of men and boys. In such cases the musical difficulties that ensue are often of the most discouraging nature, the distance between choir and organ making it next to impossible to render a smooth and artistic service.

Instead of taking the old organ down and setting it up again in a different position (possibly not suited to it), a better plan is to sell it, and have a new one built expressly designed for chancel use. When funds are wanting to either move the organ or build a new one (and if a vested choir be not yet organized), it may be wise to retain the old form of choir, postponing the introduction of chorister-boys to a more advantageous period. A chancel choir without a chancel organ is an anomaly.

CHOIR-ROOM.

A well-equipped choir rehearsal-room is of great importance. Such a room should be large, light, and
above all *well ventilated.*
Impure air affects singers very quickly, causing fa-

PLAN SUGGESTED FOR CHOIR-ROOM.

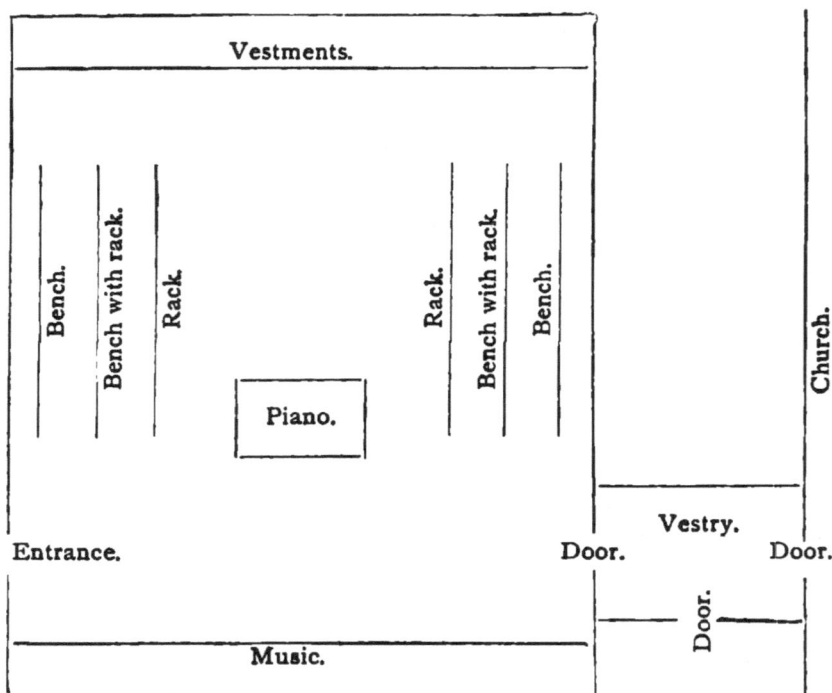

tigue, and uncertainty of pitch. The choir-room should
be furnished with a piano (*not an upright*), comfort-
able benches with music-racks attached, book-cases for
the music, and a vestment-closet. A piano is prefer-
able to a reed organ for training purposes, because it
is an instrument of percussion, speaks quickly, and is

free from the wheezing noise peculiar to the latter—a matter of importance, as boys are apt to imitate the tone quality of the instrument. The benches should have music-racks attached with a *two-inch* ledge to prevent the music from slipping off. Choir benches are sometimes needlessly uncomfortable, especially when the backs are improperly shaped, or when the music-racks project too far, cutting the shoulders or necks of the choristers, and compelling them to sit in a stooping position. The piano should be placed at one end of the room, with the benches on both sides, and the music and vestment-closets at either end.

When the choir is very large, and there is space enough, the vestment-closet may be extended around the sides of the room.

This closet should be provided with additional hooks for coats, and an upper shelf for hats. There are various kinds of vestment-closets : some are made with folding doors, some with sliding doors, and others with sliding curtains. The plan of having a separate locker, of ample dimensions, for each member of the choir, is to be commended for some reasons.

An inexpensive, convenient, and simple form of vestment-closet is made by running a shelf across an end or side of the room, about five feet above the floor, with supports where needed. Pendent from this shelf, on the under side, are double screw hooks (two for each chorister) numbered. About a foot above this shelf, runs a similar one, forming with the first an intervening space for hats. A brass rod is attached to the upper shelf, supporting sliding curtains. Thus each chorister has accommodation for his cassock and cotta, and his coat and hat.

Folding doors take up too much space if the choir-room be small. Sliding doors cut off one section of the closet while opening another. The curtains are free from either of these objections.

When there is a separate robing-room, no vestment-closet is needed. It is, however, highly desirable that the movements of the choir take place under the eye of the choir-master, *in one large room*, as it causes more or less trouble to rehearse in one part of a building, robe in another, and form the line of procession in still another. The less space the movements of the choir cover, the better for discipline and general expedition.

To fully understand the convenience of such a room (see diagram), let us suppose it to be nearly service time, and the choristers to be assembling in the choir-room. As each one enters at the side door, he goes to the numbered hook assigned him, places his hat on the shelf directly above, unhooks his cassock and cotta, hangs up his coat in their place, robes, and takes his seat. The choir-master or his assistant surveys everything at a single glance. There is no running in and out of different rooms, and no chance for confusion. The entire choir can robe and be seated in a twinkling, ready for the processional hymn, and ready to receive any final hints from the choir-master regarding the performance of the service. When the time for service arrives, the choristers being already seated in the same relative positions that they will occupy in the chancel, there is no need of forming the "processional" line. After the prayer, the hymn having been given out on the piano (which must be in tune with church organ), the choristers commence singing, and march out through the vestry-room into the church, the clergy falling into line after them.

To call attention to all this detail of choir movements may seem superfluous to the uninitiated, yet it is in reality a very important point. In cases where the vestry is used as a robing-room, not only is the choirmaster hindered, but the clergy are disturbed and annoyed by the choristers. Most rectors desire the vestry-room to be private.

In some churches the choir have to pass in and out of passages, up and down narrow stairways, robe in some out-of-the-way room, rehearse sometimes in the basement and sometimes in the Sunday school-room, and in cases of pre-occupation they cannot rehearse at all.

The choir-room should be reserved for the exclusive use of the choir-master and his singers. It is frequently necessary to coach both boys and men privately, and at any time, whenever they can take their lessons. It is a decided help to a choir-master to be able to resort to his choir-room whenever occasion requires, without danger of interruption, and without feeling that he is trespassing upon the rights of the "sewing-school" or the "infant class."

CARE OF THE MUSIC.

Hymnals, chant books, oratorios, etc., may be kept in ordinary shelved book-cases. For anthems (most of them are of Novello's octavo size) a special closet must be made, with divisions pocketed off and numbered, one division for each set of anthems. Copies can thus be kept in better order than if tied up in packages and placed away on shelves—a process involving loss of time and wear and tear. This closet should be carefully made, and should have close-fitting doors to prevent the entrance of dust. Anthems should never be used *uncovered.* They should be sent immediately upon purchase to a binder, and should be well stitched into stout manila covers. The edges should then be machine cut. This is all very inexpensive, costing only about one cent per copy, and *saving in the end the expense of replacing worn out music.*

The best method of labelling and numbering the copies is by means of rubber-faced type, which can be had at any stationer's. These type are movable, and are made to fit small metallic frames. When a new anthem comes in from the bindery, the choir-librarian should set its number and title in type, stamp the entire set, and consign it to its proper pocket in the closet. For example,

"863. SAVIOUR OF SINNERS. MENDELSSOHN."

On the left side of each set of anthems should be kept the librarian's copy, on which should be marked the number of copies in the set.

In putting away the music after any service or rehearsal, the librarian can refer to his own copy for the right number, count the copies, and thus make sure that none are missing. Otherwise it is impossible to keep trace of the number of copies in each set, as they may be mislaid, lost, or taken from the library without the knowledge of the librarian.

A complete catalogue of the music should be kept in the choir-room for reference.

Manuscript music is something to be avoided, if possible, as there is nothing more difficult to keep in order. If but little of it is needed, the best plan is to have it copied into strongly bound books made for the purpose. When much copying is necessary, the " hecktograph," " autocopyist," or "papyrograph," should be called into use (the hecktograph is the simplest), the copying sheets cut anthem size, and (after the impression is taken) bound in manila, and labelled like the anthems. Loose sheets of manuscript are not only troublesome to the librarian, but soon get soiled, torn, and ragged.

SUPPLY OF MUSIC.

A scant supply of music copies is a fatal drawback to any choir. Choristers cannot pay strict attention to their work if they are obliged to look over each other's music, nor will the music last long if subjected to the "sharing" process. Unless each member of the choir has his own copy to sing from, trouble is likely to follow.

CHOIR-LIBRARIAN.

The duty of the choir-librarian is to take strict care of all the music, and to be able to render an " account of his stewardship" at any time. An indolent, careless person cannot be taught to do this, and some one who is industrious, methodical, and who will take pride in the library should be chosen.

CARE OF THE VESTMENTS.

Choir vestments are generally taken care of by a committee of ladies, appointed for the purpose. The robes ought to be examined every week, repaired, and kept in complete and constant order. Carelessness in this department of parochial work tells disastrously

3

upon the appearance of the choir in church. Torn or soiled robes should never be used in Divine Service. The vestments should be numbered with detachable pieces of linen, indelibly marked, and a list should be kept upon a silicate slate, framed and hung in a convenient place for reference. It is advisable to have some one superintend the robing of the choir before service.

CHANCEL ACCOMMODATIONS.

The chancel choir-stalls should be designed not merely with regard to appearance, but to comfort as well. When a choir is crowded into too small a space, uneasiness and disorder ensue, detrimental to efficient singing. It is a matter of regret that chancels, even those expressly built for the accommodation of vested choirs, are often *too small.* Choir-stalls, when made with regard to comfort, take up more room than is generally allowed. There is nothing more fatiguing than kneeling for any length of time under cramped conditions. Yet in the appointments of many chancels, the comfort of the choir would seem to be the last thing thought of.

Critical members of the congregation who sit in well-cushioned seats and kneel (?) on soft hassocks, are sometimes loud in their complaints about the restlessness of choristers. They do not always take into consideration the amount of physical exertion necessary to kneel, with body erect and motionless, through the longer parts of the service, and they expect children to perform a duty without sign of fatigue which *they* will not always attempt.

CHAPTER III.

CHARACTERISTICS OF THE BOY VOICE.

PRIOR to the age of puberty, the voice of the boy is anatomically and physiologically like that of the girl. The growth and development of the larynx in each goes on in the same way, being comparatively rapid for the first six years, and then ceasing until puberty. From the sixth to the fifteenth year the larynx remains in an unchanging condition, neither enlarging nor developing to any appreciable extent. After puberty, the resemblance between the two voices disappears. With the physical changes inaugurated at that period, comes a second rapid growth of the boy's larynx, while that of the girl alters but slightly.

"At the time of puberty, which generally takes place at the age of fourteen or fifteen, but sometimes a couple of years sooner or later, the larynx grows rapidly during a period of from six months to two or three years, until it attains its final size.

"In boys it alters in the proportions of from 5 to 10, and in girls from 5 to 7.

"The larynx is at this time more or less red, and the tissue loose ; the vocal ligaments increase not only in length but also in thickness. In boys the shield cartilage loses the gentle curve, and forms the prominence which goes under the name of ' Adam's apple ; ' the larynx in its entirety increases more in depth than in height, with the result of adding to the length of the vocal ligaments, thereby producing lower tones. In girls, the larynx increases more in height than in depth and width, and the horizontal outline of the shield does not lose its evenness." (B. 66.) The peculiar "break" noticeable in a boy's voice while changing, is familiar to all. The reason assigned for it is the uneven growth of the muscles and cartilages of the larynx. The former develop slower than the latter during pubescence, and thus the normal relation of the parts necessary for vocalization is temporarily disturbed.

While there is no anatomical or physiological difference between the voices of boys and girls, there is an *acquired* difference in *timbre*, which, although slight in many cases, can be detected by a discriminating ear. The conversational tone of a girl's voice is usually softer and more musical than that of a boy's.* In singing, the difference is more apparent. Girls, especially those who live under refining influences, sing with a comparatively pure quality of tone, defective of course from lack of training, but nevertheless possessing a pure and agreeable quality.

The singing of boys, on the other hand, is coarse and (excepting in the case of trained choristers) positively disagreeable. This difference in quality is *acquired* in boys by their habitual forcing and straining of their lower, or "thick," vocal registers.

In order to understand this matter more fully, it is necessary to investigate the meaning of the term "register."

* There are, however, numerous exceptions to the rule. Rough and boisterous girls acquire harsh, discordant voices ; while quiet boys of musical instincts, have pure and musical voices. (?.)

"*A register consists of a series of tones which are produced by the same mechanism.*" (E. 86.) Laryngoscopy has proved that the vocal bands in the larynx, or voice-box, undergo a marked change in their vibratory action for different series of notes. By "mechanism," in the above definition, is meant the action of the larynx, which produces *different sets of vibrations ;* and by "register" is meant the range of voice confined to a given set of vibrations. In passing the voice from one register to another, the larynx changes its mechanism, and calls into play a different form of vibration.

There are, broadly speaking, *two* vocal registers, the "thick" and the "thin."

Browne and Behnke, in their great work entitled "Voice, Song, and Speech," subdivide these into "lower thick," "upper thick," "lower thin," "upper thin," and "small." These subdivisions, are however, of little practical value in the training of choir-boys.

The terms "thick" and "thin" were first suggested by Curwen, on the ground that they conveyed a physical meaning not expressed by the arbitrary names, "head," "chest," "throat," "upper," "lower," "medium," etc.—terms commonly met with in treatises on singing.

Notes sung in the *thick* register are produced by the vocal bands vibrating "in their entire length, breadth, and *thickness.*" When notes are sung in the thin register, only the "*thin inner edges* of the vocal bands vibrate." Hence the terms.

Boys use and develop the thick register more than the other. In fact, they seldom know of the existence of the thin register, unless the use of it is taught them by singing-masters.

A keen musical ear is all that is necessary to distinguish between the two registers. With the exception
of the break between the so-called "chest" and "falsetto" registers of the tenor, there is no vocal transition
so marked as that from the thick to the thin register
in the boy.

Nevertheless, there are many musical people who
experience more or less difficulty in this matter. "We
can take a horse to the water, but we cannot make him
drink ; and we can give a man the opportunity of
listening to the registers in a voice, but we cannot
make him hear them." (B. 178.)

Take an untrained boy to the piano and ask him to
sing *as loud as he can* up the scale to 𝄞. Now
tell him to sing 𝄞 *piano*, and note the change,
not in *power* but in *quality*.

The process may be reversed. Make him sing from
𝄞 *piano* down to 𝄞 (insist upon quiet singing). Now tell him to sing 𝄞 as loud as he can,
and the change in *timbre* will be apparent. The point
of transition will not always correspond with the above,
being sometimes higher and sometimes lower.

The quality of the thick register is comparatively
coarse, harsh, and reedy, while that of the thin is soft,
pure, and flute-like. This difference in timbre can be
imitated after a fashion by playing upon the church
organ the following scale, using a reed stop on the
swell, and a soft flute on the great, thus :

It will be noticed that the point of transition in ascending the scale is higher than in descending. This is generally the case, the thick register being forced upward, and the thin carried below the preceding break. Curwen says, " If we take a dozen untrained boys and try their voices one by one, the result is misleading. The boys are timid. Being timid they sing softly, and change early into the thin register. The best way of noticing the natural habits of boys' voices is to make a company of them sing all together up the scale of C, beginning at the C between the two clefs. If they are told to sing loudly, the break will be all the more marked. When they reach A (second space of treble staff) the change will be perceptible in a very few, but as each higher note is reached, the forced and harsh tones of the thick register will drop out more and more, leaving the clear and soft tones of the thin register. Everyone who tries this experiment, carrying the voices up to the G above the treble staff, will be at once convinced of the change of register. There will of course be a great difference among the voices. Some will instinctively change at the proper places and will show an even quality throughout ; others will be poor and husky, apparently almost without the thin register. If the choir-master can pick and choose, he will naturally take those boys who already seem to know how to use their voices, and reject the others. Our aim, however, is rather to help those who have to take the material they can get. It is certainly the greater triumph to cure boys with bad habits than simply to accept those with good ones." (G. 149.) The frequent use of the thick register is noticeable not only in the singing of

boys, but even in their speaking. It is perfectly
natural that this should be the case. Boys live, to a
great extent, out-door, " rough and tumble " lives, and
no small part of their time is spent in athletic pursuits,
in which they shout and yell vociferously.* They form
from early childhood the habit of not only forcing and
straining the thick register, but of *continually using it.*

Girls do the same to a mild extent, but they do not
carry their abuse of the vocal organs nearly so far as
boys do. They are more gently disposed, less given
to boisterous out-door games, and consequently use
their voices more quietly, and employ the thin register
more frequently. The word "abuse" here does not
mean positive injury to the voice. We seldom hear of
boys damaging their voices, no matter how hard they
play, or how loud they yell. But speaking from a
musical standpoint, *it is abuse*, for it brings the voice
into such an unsingable condition as to defy at times
the efforts of the most skilful voice-trainer.†

* " Rough play in noisy streets, attended by loud shouting, I find to
be, through forcing the tones of the lower register, the most frequent
cause of failure in training boys' voices ; so boys of superior classes
make the best singers."—E. H. TURPIN, F.C.O. (F. 21.)

† See preface for Mr. Curwen's graphic description of a carelessly
trained choir.

CHAPTER IV.

IN the vocal management of choir-boys, the difficulty that persistently asserts itself is their tendency
to fall back into their accustomed rough method of
using their voices. To overcome this tendency requires constant and unremitting care on the teacher's
part. In the cathedral choir-schools of England the —
choristers seldom hear anything but good singing, and
this fact alone acts as a preventive of voice deterioration. The boys live, so to speak, in an atmosphere of
pure vocalization. The state of things is far different
with other choirs, and particularly with American
choirs. In this country the choristers are generally
pupils in the public schools, and are obliged to sing
daily with the rest of their classmates the usual school
singing exercises. They are thus brought into daily
contact with the worst kind of vocal intonation, and
unconsciously imitate the coarse singing of their school-
mates. The effect upon their voices as regards timbre
is necessarily injurious in the highest degree. "Children, even more than adults, are influenced through
the voice. . . . The ear in childhood develops so
rapidly that impressions are received and habits formed
which it is difficult to eradicate in after-years." (F. 36.)

" That special skill and care are required in a teacher
who has in charge the voices of children, there can be

no question. But unhappily no regard is paid to this consideration in the system of teaching singing in the schools. . . . To any teacher who can sing at all, or play on any instrument, the tender voices of children are entrusted." (C. 175.)

In fitting boys for choir-work, the first thing to be done is to modify the coarseness of the thick register by extending the thin register downward. An attempt will be made to give in detail a method of beginning the training of new boys, which may also be used for re-training a badly taught choir. The rector of a parish once exclaimed to the writer, " Choir-manuals often speak casually of 'vocal registers,' etc., and the importance of 'careful training,' but such information misses the mark. No definite starting-point is assigned to the tyro in voice training. *A detailed plan of procedure is needed to effect any good."* The reader must bear in mind, however, that when he clearly understands the *vocal principles* set forth in these pages, he may not confine himself to any set method of practice.

The boys, being assembled in a class, should be taught to sing *sustained notes.* Thus :

Ah,   ah,   ah,   ah.

each note being held for a few seconds, and accompanied on the pianoforte with simple* harmonies. The choristers should be taught separately at first, and when several succeed in producing the right quality of tone, they may sing together. In beginning with a class of " raw recruits" it is a good plan to make those

---

* Do not strive for elaborate harmonies ; look to the voices.

who learn quickly stand on one side of the room, and those whose voices do not yield readily to treatment stand on the opposite side. As soon as the slow ones improve, they may be promoted to the first side. Commencing now with the note ♪ (or any note high enough to be beyond the reach of the thick register), let the chorister with the best voice sing Italian a (ah, like a in "father"), taking strict care that the note be sung *piano* and in the thin register (a point to be decided by the ear of the teacher). If properly sung, let another boy join in and sing with the first, both keeping the note *soft* and *pure*. Proceeding with boy after boy in this way, nearly all will sing the note with the proper register. Those who fail, and sing the note badly, by forcing up the thick register (as yet they will be few, as the note is too high), should be sent to the opposite side before mentioned. The contrast between the tone quality of the two sides thus formed will be apparent even to the boys themselves.

Care must be taken with each chorister that his breathing be full and easy, his mouth well open, his lips parted sufficiently to let the sound pass the teeth, and his tongue lying quietly in its proper place, hollowed like the bowl of a spoon.

Proceed down the scale by semi-tones, following carefully the above method. After passing ♪ take particular care that the timbre does not change, because now the boys may begin a very coarse quality and break into the thick register. As the scale descends, it will become more and more difficult to confine them to the proper register, and upon arrival at ♪

they will probably all sing with a strong mixture of
coarse, thick tone.* Do not go below 𝄞⎯⎯ at first,
but return to the top of the scale again, and repeat the
process just gone through. It is of primary importance that the notes be sung *very softly* and with *full* and
easy breathing. Otherwise but little progress will be
made in blending the registers. Bring the voices down
the scale again and again, slowly and carefully, with
piano singing. After a little practice the boys on the opposite side will see what is wanted and imitate the quiet
tone of the others. By patient and persistent adher-
ence to this method of training, the above compass may
be extended, and the whole class will eventually learn to
produce a perfectly pure and even intonation throughout the entire range from 𝄞⎯⎯ to 𝄞⎯⎯.

" It must be remembered that the voice of a perfect
singer shows no recognizable break or line of division
between the vocal registers. . . . . One great end
sought to be attained by vocal training in singing is to
make the voice as nearly as possible uniform throughout the extent of its range."—*Dr. Austin Flint.*

After the use of the thin register is thoroughly acquired, it is better to practise the voices *up* the scale instead of down, care being taken to avoid extremes. *It is
also advisable to begin the practice of chants and hymns in a
high key, lowering them by semi-tones until they reach their
original pitch.* In singing low notes, the tendency to

---

* In teaching individual voices this scale exercise, it is a good plan to
stop the instant the break is detected, make the pupil return to the
top of the scale again, and descend with greater care and attention to
the break.

break into the coarse, thick quality is far greater than in singing high notes. The more the upper part of the voice is exercised, the quicker the use of the thin register will be acquired. The chief points involved in the preceding directions are : 1st, downward extension of the thin register ; 2d, the cultivation of pure tone without sacrificing quality to power.

The singing of the celebrated choir at St. Cunnibert's, Cologne, is thus described in Browne and Behnke's work on " The Child's Voice : " " It seems to be far from Vicar Hoeveler's object to secure a large volume of sound. All his attention is devoted to the quality of tone, which is indeed in his choir something altogether special. *The head* voice only is used,* even by the altos, down to their lowest notes, or very nearly so. The boys are taught to take breath silently and swiftly, not very much, apparently, but very frequently. The accented and unaccented words and syllables are very carefully observed, and the understanding between choir and director is most intimate. The result of this training is a quality of tone so soft, velvety, mysterious, as we have never heard before ; a perfect intonation, a wonderful evenness of voice from top to bottom of their range, freedom from shrillness in the upper notes, and from roughness in the middle."

Mr. Curwen gives the following account of the famous choir of the Temple Church, London (Dr. E. J. Hopkins, organist and choir-master) : " With a choir of twelve boys and six men, Mr. Hopkins realizes his ideas of 'quality, not quantity.' The two Honorable Societies of the Temple pay liberally for their music,

* The term "head" voice is in common use. Head notes are those sung in the thin register.

hence they command as good voices as the cathedrals
. . . At the Sunday service the ear of the listener is
arrested by the smoothness and blending of the general
effect. It is the purest art. Mr. Hopkins knows the
power of soft music over the emotions, how the spirit
of the worshipper yields to the still, small voice, when
thunder and declamation fail to touch. With a choir
which can float without support, unnumbered effects in
accompaniment are possible. . . . . In point of
choir-training, the voices of the boys must naturally ex-
cite the attention of choir-masters. Their sweetness
and fulness, the agility with which they attack the notes,
their strength and clearness in the region which lies
from D to F at the top of their voices, are alike remarkable. There is neither rattle nor strain ; all is pure tone,
and the power of the soprano part gives brightness to
all the music."

Dr. E. J. Hopkins is quoted as saying (G. 163):
" Nowadays every one is for quantity, not quality, and
coarseness is the prevailing vice. We are told of surpliced choirs of thirty-six voices, and if we go to hear
them, what do we too frequently find ? A great racket
and shouting, certainly, but not music."

Emil Behnke, in his "Mechanism of the Human
Voice," says, " *Never extend lower registers upward, but
strengthen the upper registers and carry them downward, thus
equalizing the voices from top to bottom and enabling your
pupils to sing without straining.*" (E. 104.) Behnke empha-
sizes this, and dwells upon it at some length, declaring
that it is the most important lesson taught in his book.
Again he says: "The carrying down of a register causes
no fatigue, and though its volume is weak as compared
with the corresponding lower register, it is surprising

how soon it can, by judicious practice, be made to acquire fulness and power." (E. 103.)

The standard writers on the voice are loud in their denunciation of singing teachers who neglect this law ; much could here be quoted on the subject from the works of Madame Emma Seiler and others, did space permit.

The immediate result of this system of training is *temporary lack of vocal strength.* The force and " staying power " of a choir apparently vanish when first the use of the thin register is insisted upon. This often leads to ignorant but severe criticism, and in many cases choir-masters who have been struggling to free their choristers from their harsh, thick tones, grow disheartened, give up, and let their boys slip back into their old habits of singing, rather than contend against adverse opinion. In such cases the rule must be "nil desperandum." The soft, pure tones of the thin register develop slowly but *surely.* The clear, resonant "ring" of the voice on high notes, and the soft, mellow quality on low ones, is only to be secured by *patient* training. It is easier to make water run up hill than to drive and hurry the voice. Nature takes her own time. She will consent to be coaxed, and slowly led step by step, but never will be hurried.

"Purity in the art of singing is, however, such a primal condition of its beauty, that a piece of music purely executed, even by a weak and slightly cultivated voice, always sounds agreeably, while the most sonorous and practised voice offends the hearer when it is out of tune or *forced upward.*" (C. 138.)

CHAPTER V.

BREATHING, RESONANCE, ATTACK, AND FLEXI-BILITY.

AT every rehearsal, the first fifteen or twenty min-utes should be given to the practice of exercises for the equalization of the registers, and for the *development* of the voice. It is not the *number* of exercises, but the *method of singing* them, that chiefly concerns us. The practice of the scale by sustained notes, as suggested in the previous chapter, is the most useful exercise for general purposes. When a variety of exercises is de-sired, they may either be invented to suit the wants of the choristers, or a selection may be made from the numberless vocalises in the various manuals of singing. After the use of the thin register has been acquired, the voices should be developed, as far as possible, by attention to Breathing, Resonance, Attack, and Flexi-bility. To do more than outline the salient points under each of these four topics is here impossible. To enlarge fully upon them would be to go beyond the province of this work. The time spent upon the vocal training of choir-boys is so short, and they are so gen-erally taught by *class teaching*, that it becomes impos-sible to utilize to a full extent all the teachings of vocal science. It should, nevertheless, be the earnest en-deavor of every choir-master, entrusted with the train-ing of young voices, to become familiar with the funda-

mental laws governing the voice, and in his teaching
to obey those laws to the best of his ability.

BREATHING.

" There are three ways of carrying on the process of
respiration, namely, midriff breathing, rib breathing,
and collar-bone breathing.   These three ways are not
indeed wholly independent of each other ; they over-
lap or partly extend into each other.   Nevertheless,
they are sufficiently distinct, and it is a general and
convenient practice to give to each a separate name,
according to the means by which it is chiefly called
into existence.   The combined forms of midriff and
of rib breathing constitute the right way, and collar-
bone breathing is totally wrong and vicious, and should
not in a state of health be made use of under any circumstances.

" When enlarging our chests by the descent of the
midriff, we inflate the lungs where they are largest, and
where consequently we can get the largest amount of
air into them.   When expanding our chests by raising
the shoulders and collar-bones, we inflate the lungs
where they are smallest, and where consequently we
get the smallest amount of air into them.

" *The criterion of correct inspiration is an increase of size
of the abdomen and of the lower part of the chest.   Who-
ever draws in the abdomen and raises the upper part of the
chest, breathes wrongly.*"   (B. 138 and 142.)

Carelessness in regard to hygienic breathing is common enough among adults.   Among choir-boys it is
universal.   They not only breathe by raising the
shoulders and filling the upper part of the chest, but
they breathe *hurriedly* and *insufficiently*, only partially

4

filling the lungs, and often taking barely enough breath
to sustain a note more than a second or two. To overcome bad habits of breathing, it is best to explain to
each chorister separately the proper method, and then
watch all as carefully as possible during rehearsals, to
see that they practise full abdominal breathing. " The
air is the motive power upon which the voice depends ;
without air no tone can be produced."

Absolute control of the breath is consequently a
point of vital importance. Choristers should be taught
to breathe deliberately, to fill the lungs without over-
crowding them, and to *economize the expiration of breath
by not allowing it to rush through the larynx without doing
its full work.* " Every particle of air sent forth while
singing must be employed in generating sound "
(Randegger). " The singer Delle Sedie runs up and
down the scale before a flame, and it never wavers. This
is because he permits only the exact amount of breath
to escape which is requisite to force the sound straight-
forward, and the air being thus occupied in the emission of the note, loses its quality of wind, and is reduced to its quality of sound."

An easy erect position of the body, with head and
shoulders well back, is all-important. A stooping or
lolling posture is fatal to proper breathing and voice
delivery. It should be remembered that boys are in a
condition of growth. Their frames cannot contain the
same amount of air as in the case of an adult. They
should be allowed to breathe rather frequently. Care
should be taken not to tax their breathing powers, and
to avoid extremes, both in inspiration and expiration.
In practising sustained notes, the breathing capacity
should be slowly and carefully increased. After a

time the notes may be held for eight or ten seconds, if
no fatigue is caused. Steady progress in control of
breath can be judiciously gained from this single
exercise.

RESONANCE.

Vocal sound is first *produced* by the air sent from the
lungs to the larynx, past the vocal bands, which are
thereby set in vibration. The sound is then *modified*
by the pharynx, the mouth, and the nose. If these
parts, which modify sound, be skilfully managed,
reinforcement and *resonance* of tone result. If, on the
other hand, they are badly managed, clear emission of
tone is interfered with. The subject of resonance is a
broad one, and there are many scientific truths in
connection with it which we cannot practically apply
in class training. By attention to some of the more
important points, however, much good may result.
First of all, a correct position of the mouth should be
insisted upon. Many choristers persist in half closing
the mouth, and singing with a slovenly, muffled quality
of tone. Others will sing with the teeth nearly touch-
ing, producing a noise similar to that made by singing
through a comb. Such habits are difficult to cure. In
opening the mouth, the lower jaw should not be rigidly
projected, but moved quietly and easily ; indeed, the
whole facial expression should be pleasant and natural, the lips should not cover the teeth too much, or
resonance will suffer. The tone should leave the
upper part of the mouth *unmuffled*, which cannot hap-
pen if the lips are drawn over the teeth. This is the
reason why a smiling expression is sometimes recommended by singing masters. A *clear forward* tone
should be striven for, and the voice directed toward

the upper part of the mouth and toward the front, thus utilizing the roof of the mouth (hard palate) as a sounding board. *Hard blowing* and *violent singing, instead of increasing the reach of the voice,* lessen it. It is a common sight to see a choir-boy working away with all his might, red in the face with over-exertion and over-blowing. Such muscular singing is utterly destructive of pure delivery. *The power and reach of the voice should depend chiefly upon forward reflection of tone, and absolute purity of timbre and articulation.* " Let the tone come well forward in the mouth and try to keep it there. If you have a feeling as though it went away from you and you had to run after it to catch it, it will never be a telling tone. Sing *softly* but *vigorously,* and above all things sing *beautifully."* "Work for quality, and power will take care of itself." (B. 172.)

Nasal tone is caused by the falling of the soft palate, partially closing the exit through the mouth, and diverting the tone through the nose. The cure for it is tedious, and consists in the practice of exercise for controlling the muscles of the palate. Catarrh often is at the root of the trouble. It is not worth while to bother with a boy who has a marked nasal twang. If admitted to the choir through oversight, he should be allowed to resign. The choir-room should not be turned into a vocal hospital. Nasal tone is often associated with throaty tone, when the tongue rises at its root, shutting in the sound and allowing it to pass through the nose.

A common fault in boy singing is *throatiness.* This defect is a very noticeable one, the singer, apparently, trying to generate and deliver his voice entirely in his closed throat, without the least regard to the action of lungs, larynx, or the parts affecting resonance.

The larynx then rises *too high*, the throat becomes partially contracted and closed, and the vocal *timbre* radically impaired.

In singing, the voice-box naturally alters its position in the throat according to pitch.

When the pitch ascends, the larynx ascends, and *vice versa*. This motion can be distinctly felt. Place the tip of the finger lightly upon the front of the larynx, and sing a low note. The larynx descends. Now sing a high note, and it will fly upward, and slip away from the finger entirely. To try to prevent the larynx from rising *at all* is of course wrong, but it should not rise *too high*. In singing high notes, if a sensation is experienced as though the notes were cramped and sticking in the throat, the singer should endeavor to rid himself of it by generating the notes lower down, and by thus opening the throat. (What is here said refers to the *sensation* felt in singing. Strictly speaking, the point of generation is nowhere else but in the larynx, at the vocal bands.) "There is in all beginners a tendency to sing too much in the head, *that, is to have the formation of the tones too high up in the throat.* This fault is due to the difficulty experienced by beginners in keeping the larynx sufficiently below the mouth. The fulness of tone, the rich, round, and mellow quality which is so much admired in all good singers, is almost entirely owing to the voice being pitched *low down*, and not high up in the throat, toward the back of the head (as it appears to be)." (D. 58.) Hasty, careless, and insufficient breathing is a fruitful cause of throatiness. Without proper breathing there is poor control of air,

and when there is poor control of air, everything connected with voice delivery necessarily suffers. Another
cause of throatiness is the rising of the tongue at its
base, shutting in the sound. Boys should be taught to
keep the tongue *out of the way*, by allowing it to rest
quietly in the bottom of the mouth, hollowed like the
bowl of a spoon.

"It is admitted by all authorities, without exception,
that the production of a good vocal tone necessitates—
1st, a supple, open throat ; 2d, bringing the tone well
forward in the mouth. It is precisely in these two
fundamental requirements that singers frequently en-
counter the greatest difficulty. The throat stiffens,
the root of the tongue does likewise, the throat nar-
rows, the tone is *shut in*, and all its beauty is destroyed."

ATTACK.

The larynx during inspiration, when it is not employed in phonation, allows the vocal bands to separate, and the glottis is then *open*. The instant expiration and phonation commence, the vocal bands
approximate and the glottis is *closed*. In the production of a tone, the closing muscles affecting the vocal
bands are called into play.

When phonation ceases and inspiration begins, the
opening muscles are used. An exercise suggested by
Browne and Behnke (B. 151) consists in singing a
number of short notes, *each note being preceded by a short
inspiration*. Thus,

In singing such a series of notes the glottis is alter-
nately opened and closed, tones are commenced and

ended, and the muscles thereby involved are exercised to an infinitely greater extent than in singing sustained notes.

In correct "attack" the vocal ligaments meet just at the very moment when the air strikes against them. They are not pressed together more tightly than necessary. No preliminary escape of air takes place. The attack is clear and decisive, and the tone consequently gets a proper start. (B. 128.)

This exercise is of decided value, especially in getting rid of the sliding, "scooping" habit of attack which many boys have, and which is often very difficult to cure.

Mental attention plays an important part in suddenly attacking a high note, especially if preceded by a long pause. The pitch of the note should be *thought of* before the attack is made.

FLEXIBILITY.

Vocal flexibility is to be acquired chiefly by faithful and continuous practice, and it may be truthfully said that few singers, even among the adult professional ranks, possess it in a high degree.

"Execution is certainly one of the most difficult parts of musical science. Young singers are desirous of attaining it without reflecting whether, from the formation of the throat and various physical causes, they may ever be able to accomplish their wishes. Few indeed possess the power of execution in a pre-eminent degree. It is in part a gift of Nature, and those who have ever delighted as well as astonished us by their rapid manner of running through divisions must have been naturally endowed with flexible organs." (D. 105.)

Fortunately, the music which choir-boys are called upon to sing, generally makes but moderate demands upon flexibility. It is chiefly in the soprano solos of the more elaborate anthems that passages of unusual brilliancy and rapidity occur. Let us briefly consider what vocal flexibility means. In phonation, the vocal bands are placed upon the stretch. Whenever the pitch *ascends*, the tension of the bands increases, and when the pitch descends, their tension diminishes. When a singer can relax or contract with *rapidity and precision the vocal muscles governing pitch*, his voice is said to be flexible.

Such flexibility of voice can be acquired only by the persevering practice of exercises on the rapid change of pitch. In teaching a class of boys exercises in flexibility, we cannot expect great results, excepting in cases where they can be rehearsed every day, or twice a day. For ordinary uses the following exercises, *practised in various keys*, will be found useful.

All exercises on flexibility should be practised at first *slowly, softly, distinctly,* giving each note a slight accent, and thus preventing the blurred effect commonly heard in the singing of rapid passages. *The tempo must not be increased at the expense of distinctness.*

CHAPTER VI.

Two varieties of altos are used for choir purposes, the counter-tenor and the boy alto. The counter-tenor voice is thus spoken of in Grove's "Dictionary of Music and Musicians," "Alto (from the Latin altus, high, far removed). The male voice of the highest pitch, called also counter-tenor, *i.e.*, *contra*, or against the tenor. In the 16th and early part of the 17th centuries, the compass of the alto voice was limited to the notes admissible on the stave which has the C clef on its third line, *i.e.*, to the notes a sixth above and a sixth below middle C. Later, however, this compass was extended by bringing into use the third register of the voice, or falsetto, a register often strongest with those whose voices are naturally bass.

"The falsetto counter-tenor, or more properly speaking, counter-alto, still to be found in cathedral choirs, dates, if musical history is to be read in music, from the restoration of Charles II., who doubtless desired to reproduce at home, approximately at least, a class of voice he had become accustomed to in continental chapels, royal and ducal."

The counter-tenor voice, although extensively employed in England, is as yet but little known in this country. It is liable to much unjust criticism here, as people are unaccustomed to it, and are prone to regard

it as an innovation and novelty. Another cause opera-
ting against the popularity of the voice is that its cultivation is often sadly neglected. Many of the adult
altos in our choirs are careless in their vocal methods.
Their singing could be immeasurably improved by
painstaking practice. Such singers should remember
that, if it is worth while to sing alto at all, it is worth
while to sing it well.

The capabilities of the voice are greater than is generally supposed, and much can be accomplished by judicious training.* There is a prevailing impression,
founded upon prejudice, that it is injurious to the
vocal organs to sing falsetto. Injury to the voice (no
matter what kind of voice) comes from over-exercise,
straining, and carelessness in exceeding the limits of the
registers. If the falsetto register be developed physiologically, and not subjected to abuse, no evil results
can possibly follow its employment.†

The scarcity of counter-tenors is a difficulty; but
when they are not to be *found*, they can be *made*. There
are many inferior bass and tenor voices in which the
falsetto register yields readily to training.

* Although men do not use the falsetto register in speaking, it is not
yet proved to be impossible for the male voice to attain the same results as the female.

When in the beginning the falsetto tones are sung always *piano* and
very *staccato*, by long continued, careful practice, with entirely the same
physical treatment of both registers, a smooth and natural transition
from one to the other is most easily obtained. Thus the falsetto tones
gain more and more in fulness and strength, and sound far more
agreeably than the forced-up chest tones of our tenorists, sung with
swollen-out throats and blood-red faces." (Madame Seiler, C. 72–73.)

† The author has yet to find a counter-tenor who will oppose this
view.

The main endeavor should be to make the voice sound as natural as possible, and to avoid shrillness of tone. When the break between the falsetto and the next lower register is very apparent, exercises for blending the registers should be practised.

The counter-tenor voice is held in high estimation in England, most of the cathedrals and parish churches employing it instead of the boy alto.

"The effective notes of an alto usually lie in the octave of B or B♭, and the repertoire of music for which this voice is suited is comparatively limited. That repertoire, however, includes the greater number of oratorios, a good deal of fine old Italian music, and a few old English songs ; while a singer of cleverness and cultivation will find many ballads which he may make his own by the help of transposition and style of delivery. . . . The alto in a man is totally distinct from the contralto in a woman.* The tone is utterly different. The best notes of the one are certainly not the best notes of the other. . . The low notes which are so fine in a contralto, and so unlike any other tone,

---

* "The culture and employment, as a solo instrument, of the female contralto voice, is comparatively modern, and even yet not universal. By the opera composers of France and Germany it has been, and still continues to be, but rarely employed. In his adaptation for the French theatre, of his Italian "Orfeo," originally composed, 1762, for a contralto, Gluck transposed and otherwise recast the music of the title-character for a tenor. It is to Rossini and his Italian contemporaries that the voice owes its present very important status. In few of their operas is it unemployed. In the choral music, however, of the composers of all nations it has now definitely taken its place— till lately monopolized, in England especially, by the male counter-tenor, a voice of somewhat different compass, and altogether different quality." [A, article on Contralto.]

except perhaps a few notes of some tenors, are utterly
wanting in charm, and generally in power, in a male
alto ; while the sweet and ringing middle notes of the
latter are far more effective, in alto music, than the
frequently weak and uncertain middle notes of a contralto. (D. 36.)

The real boy contralto, whose voice ranges from
to is a rarity seldom met with on this
side of the Atlantic. The boy altos usually heard in
our choirs are generally *sopranos* who have never been
taught the easy, quiet method of using the thin register,
and who sing alto by forcing and over-straining the
thick register. Clergymen and choir-masters who tol-
erate the average boy alto generally aim for "hearty"
singing (as it is called) and plenty of "vim," and care
little for purity of timbre. Such "hearty" singing is
harsh and offensive in the highest degree to cultivated
ears. Boy altos generally "bray" on their lower
coarse notes, and thus corrupt the tonal health of their
associates by setting the worst possible example of
voice delivery. There are exceptions to the rule, but
they are decidedly rare. If circumstances compel us
to utilize boys as altos, the greatest care should be
taken to treat their voices gently, and to modify the
coarseness of the thick register by extending the thin
register down as far as possible. If the tonal volume
is thus rendered weak, more voices may be added to
the part. In no case should we allow boys to strain
and shout in the lower register, for the sake of power,

at the expense of quality. Such a proceeding may be convenient, and save the trouble of training ; but it is vocally wrong, not only dulling the choristers' perception of purity of timbre, but also injuring the voices. Some choir-masters seem to admire the singing of alto boys, notwithstanding its usual defects.

Dr. Parry* is represented as saying (F. 40) : " In Wales, boys *never* did sing treble, *always alto, without exception*." (! ! !) (Italics, Dr. Parry's.) The singing of these Welsh alto boys is, however, thus referred to in " The Child's Voice " by a musical critic :

" I have been to scores of Eisteddfodau, and have seen many excellent choirs ruined by the forcing of the boy altos. I have heard many of our principal adjudicators denouncing this element in no measured terms."

Messrs. Browne and Behnke say (F. 41) : " The singing of these Welsh alto boys as above described stands in the strongest imaginable contrast with that of the boys at St. Cunnibert's, Cologne." (See page 45.) Setting aside the fact that boy altos are apt to " bray," the difficulty experienced in teaching them to read their part (especially when much elaborate music is sung), seriously augments the choir-master's labors. Furthermore, their voices must change sooner or later ; their use therefore necessitates a constant employment of new choristers. It has already been seen that the ever-recurring loss of *sopranos* constitutes the chief drawback to the employment of boy-singers ; we need not extend the same objection to altos, if we use the counter-tenor voice.

* Joseph Parry, Mus. Doc. Cantab., Principal Musical College of Wales.

CHAPTER VII.

CARELESS pronunciation not only renders it impos-sible for the listener to distinguish what is sung, but it also seriously affects vocal resonance.

Singers who distinctly articulate their words, there-by reinforce their voices, and their notes "carry" fur-ther than they otherwise would.

Choristers can learn pronunciation more readily by *imitation* than by rule, so teachers who pronounce clearly themselves, achieve the best and quickest results. It is to vowel sounds, and initial and terminal consonants, that chief attention should be given. A useful exercise consists in singing the simple sounds of A, E, I, O, U (pronounced as they are in the alphabet), successively to short notes. They should be practised with great distinctness. Afterward the modified sounds ah, aw, and oo, like a in father, aw in law, and oo in boot, should be practised. It will be found that many choristers will experience considerable difficulty in singing these eight sounds *distinctly*, and in some cases it will be hard to distinguish which sounds are sung, when the order of the vowels is changed purpose-ly to test the articulation.

All of the vowel sounds are troublesome to choris-ters. *They both mispronounce them and confuse them, using the sound of one vowel for that of another.*

A.

The American pronunciation of A is too apt to be like a in "pay." The Italian sound of a (ah) should, on account of its musical qualities, be largely used in singing. For example, in such words as "Abraham," "after," "last," "pass," etc., this broad sound of A is needed to avoid the thin non-resonant A, as in "day," etc. A definite rule on this point is difficult to make, but it is musically better to carry the use of Italian A too far than to neglect it. The diphthong in "laugh" is often sung as if the word were spelled "laff," an inexcusable mistake. In such words as "again," where the "American" sound of A *is wanted*, it is not clearly given, but changed to that of E in "pen." The word *ac*knowledge is too frequently pronounced as if spelled *ec*knowledge.

E.

This vowel is often so poorly sounded that it cannot be distinguished from I and U, especially in words like "righteousness," "wickedness," "counsel," "remembereth," "doeth," etc., which are often pronounced "righteous*nuss*," "wicked*niss*," "coun*sul*," "remember*uth*," "do*ith*," etc. "Mercy" is often sung "m*u*rcy," and "earth" "*u*rth," giving the E a U tone, as in "murmur." The word "few" is generally sounded correctly, but "dew" and "new" are likely to be corrupted into "d*oo*" and "n*oo*."

I.

The sound of I, in "evil" and similar words, is seldom clear. (Too much like ev*u*l.) In words like "vanity," i is too often sounded like A, "vanaty," "unaty," "Trinaty," etc. "V*u*rg*o*n," for v*i*rg*i*n, and "w*u*rsh*u*p" for "w*o*rsh*i*p" are common mistakes.

O.

The vowel O is ofttimes corrupted into "au" or "ou." For gl*o*ry we hear "glaury." The pure O tone should be carefully practised.

U.

It has been seen that the sound of U is sometimes given when not wanted. The reverse also happens. Choristers may sing u correctly in "commune," "rebuke," "confusion," etc.; but they *will* sing "dooty," "loot," "innoomerable," "multitood," "endoo," etc., for "duty," "lute," "innumerable," "multitude," "endue," etc.

The article "the" should be pronounced "thee" before words beginning with a vowel, and thĕ (e like u in but) before words beginning with a consonant. For example, "th*e* Anointed," "thĕ king."

When a word ending with a vowel is followed by a word beginning with a vowel, care is needed to avoid intermediate sounds. We hear in the Venite, instead of "awe of Him," an R sound between the e and the o. Again we have " Hosann*er* in " for " Hosanna in," and " endoo-*w*us " for " endue us."

Initial and terminal consonants are seldom pronounced clearly. *It is in the beginning and ending of words that careless articulation is most noticeable.* Consonant sounds must be slightly exaggerated in singing, in order to make the words intelligible. Initial and final D, T, R, and S, require special attention. We constantly hear "lor" for Lor*d*, "holy gho" for "Holy Gho*st*," "li" for "light," "fee" for "feed." Such words as trust, remember, send, etc., are generally commenced in a slovenly, indistinct manner. Final letters are ofttimes run into the following word—"rememberus" for "remember us," "thatche" for "that ye," "thatee" for "that he," "prazhee" for "praise ye," "waizeof" for "ways of," etc. Many of these examples of mispronunciation seem perhaps to be exaggerated yet they are commonly heard in choir-singing. The mistakes thus made are sometimes dreadful. The writer has heard for "O Lord, make *haste* to deliver me," "O lor, make h*a*," etc., as if "haste" were spelled "*hay*"

A habit of clear, distinct articulation can only be formed in choir-boys by constantly correcting them, not only in their singing, but also in their speaking.* The letter H, although a veritable stumbling-block to English choristers, gives the American little trouble. This is however counterbalanced by the difficulty in getting rid of the thin sound of A.

The practice of reading aloud before a critic cannot be too highly recommended as a corrective of bad pronunciation.

If choristers could avail themselves of such practice the results would be astonishing.

Bad pronunciation is particularly noticeable in *chanting*. One prolific cause of this is hurrying helter skelter over the recitation, as if it were to be gotten rid of as quickly as possible. Here are detached examples :

"Glorybetothefather," etc.,

"Asitwasinthebeginning," etc.,

"Andwithrighteousnesstojudgetheworld," etc.

* The author once heard a choir of considerable reputation sing Barnby's anthem "Break forth," etc., thus—"Break farth into jy,

5

Take for instance the sixth verse of psalm 69th. Most choirs would render it thus :

" LetnotthemthattrustinTheeOLordGodofhostsbeashamed | for . my |
    cause : letnotthosethatseekTheebeconfoundedthroughmeOLord
    | God . of | Is . ra | el."

Good chanting is like the flowing of a quiet brook. There should be no haste, no jerky effect, no hitch between verses. The words should be distinctly uttered, the slight pauses at the " holds " or commas not exaggerated, and the breathing regular and not unnecessarily frequent.

PHRASING.

" The due indication of rhythmical divisions, in *performance*, is termed phrasing, and is of great importance, though much neglected. The giving the proper stress to the accented notes, without any *jerking*, or clock-like monotony, is one element in such indication. And the dividing of the phrases is indicated, partly, by the *raising of the hand* in pianoforte playing ; by the *bowing* in stringed instrument playing ; and should regulate the *breath-taking* in singing."

The importance of teaching choristers to phrase correctly, and together, is not sufficiently appreciated. When they breathe in a " hap-hazard " fashion, not only do words and music suffer by misplaced accent, but there is a loss in steadiness of tone, caused by the irregularities of breath. To prove to boys the importance of phrasing, it is a good plan, having marked the

break farth into jy, sing tuggether ye waste places—zof Jerusalem ! "
The same choir sang vociferously in another anthem, " Hosannerin the highest, Hosannerin the highest ! ! "

breathing points in a few hymns and anthems, to teach them to breathe strictly in accordance with the marks. They will then see for themselves what phrasing means, and will realize the improvement in their singing caused by simultaneous breathing at the proper places.

"Let the performer, in singing, breathe as far as possible as he has to do in correct recitation. One breath ought to cover as many words as are required to express a complete idea. A singer should only take breath *when the musical and declamatory clauses permit*, and for this purpose he must always economize the breath at his disposal."

"Breath is to be taken at every one of the longer rests."

"The time for breathing must, where no rest is marked, always be taken from the value of the preceding, and never from that of the next, note ; because by taking it from the latter, precision in starting it could not be obtained, and time could not be properly maintained."

"Breath, when needed, must be taken at a comma, and also before the preposition introducing a prepositional clause."

"The syllables of a word must not be separated by breathing, except where necessity demands." (H. 98.)

It is well to show choristers, by means of object lessons on the blackboard, the meaning of the terms Phrase, Section, and Period ; and their analogous meaning in the division of sentences by commas. An excellent exercise is to write out a period upon the board, allowing the choristers to divide it into its constituent parts, and also to mark the breathing points. The terms phrase, section, and period are confused somewhat, and appear in different books to be inter-

changed. A period consists of two or more sections,
and a section consists of two or more phrases.

PERIOD.

SECTION.		SECTION.	
Phrase.	Phrase.	Phrase.	Phrase.

As before remarked, page 50, chorister-boys cannot
be expected to hold very much breath ; their lungs
being comparatively small and undeveloped, do not
admit of long-sustained expiration. Care, then, should
be taken to let them breathe as often as seems necessary, and not to allow them to become fatigued from
undue efforts.

EXPRESSION.

Lack of musical expression in choir-singing is largely
due to the *habit* of not paying strict attention to the
meaning of words. Unless special care is taken to
impress upon singers the importance of always understanding in their hearts what they sing with their lips,
they fall into a habit of never connecting musical with
verbal sense.

Frederick Helmore well observes, " It is not only indispensable to select appropriate music, but to give to
every sentence its real meaning by the tone of the
voice. This can only be done by a careful study of
the words, and an agreement between all the members
of a choir as to the manner in which different ideas
are to be conveyed. To this end, the following rules
for loud and soft singing have been found very useful
in calling attention to the general principles of expression."

Loud singing is expressive of	Soft singing is expressive of
Joy.	Sorrow.
Praise.	Prayer.
Righteousness.	Sin.
Vigor.	Weakness.
Rage and Fury.	Peace.
Confidence.	Fear.
Health.	Sickness.
Life.	Death.
Rewards of the righteous.	Punishments of the wicked.
Heaven.	Hell.

The *verve* and enthusiasm of a choir is greatly dependent upon the *organ accompaniment.* Dull, monotonous, lifeless playing, robs music of expression, and produces a dispiriting effect upon the singers. Too much *forte* playing is perhaps the most common fault. Loud playing, be it remembered, is not necessarily either vigorous or inspiriting. Organ accompaniment * is an *art* in itself, and should receive far more attention and study than is generally given it. Organists should particularly avoid stereotyped habits of playing.

* A very excellent little book on organ accompaniment has been written by Dr. Bridge, of Westminster Abbey. It is published by Messrs. Novello, Ewer & Co.

CHAPTER VIII.

THE average American choir receives but two rehearsals per week. The first rehearsal is generally attended by the boys only, and the second by the full choir. Some of the more notable choirs are rehearsed three times a week, while a select few receive four rehearsals weekly. The same may be said of most English choirs. It is only in cathedrals, collegiate chapels, and in parishes which support choir-schools, that choir-boys receive daily instruction.

"In places where there is daily choral service, and the music is of a high type of excellence, choir-schools are almost a necessity. The boys, living under one roof, are always available, and are practised every day, sometimes twice daily, not only in the required music, but in voice culture, exercises, and the like. But they are costly, and should not be attempted without adequate funds to support them. Excellent models of choir-schools exist in St. Paul's Cathedral; St. Mary Magdalene's, Paddington ; All Saints, Margaret Street ; King's College, Cambridge ; Magdalene College and Christ College, Oxford ; St. Michael's College, Tenbury, and other places."

It is a matter of regret that endowments are not made in America for the proper maintenance of parish choirs, and choir-schools. Until such provision is secured, we can never hope to realize in this country the same results that are attained in England.

Although circumstances do not always permit, at least three weekly rehearsals are desirable for choirs that attempt music of the better class. A choir can hardly " hold its own " with fewer rehearsals, excepting in places where very little music is expected and where musical criticism is generous.

The time of each rehearsal should not, as a rule, much exceed an hour and a half. When singers grow tired and restless, very little can be done with them. One of Richard Mann's excellent rules is, " Keep your choir in good humor with themselves ; never let them get sulky at their own failures ; rather stop with the lesson half finished."

As choirs meet for practice only two or three times a week, a point of chief importance in rehearsing is *economy of time*. Choir-masters differ wonderfully in rapidity of teaching, some accomplishing *thoroughly* in a single hour more than others accomplish *badly* in double the time. The choir-master should know beforehand exactly how he intends to spend his time, and thus avoid unnecessary delays. A service list should be made out for each month, and either printed or written copies distributed for choir use.

Before each rehearsal the choir-librarian should put on the music-racks whatever is required in the list, thus avoiding the giving out of music at rehearsals, which wastes time and causes confusion. The music can then be rehearsed systematically, and many precious minutes saved and spent upon training that would otherwise be lost in minor details.

The standing position in singing should be frequently employed. In sitting too much, boys *will* droop the head forward upon the chest, and assume various pos-

tures detrimental to voice delivery. Physically, it is a
great relief to stand a while, after sitting still for any
length of time.

A blackboard, ruled with staves, should be kept in
the choir-room for teaching sight-reading, etc. The
mere practice of the music necessary for the Sunday
services in itself teaches reading, but in inexperienced
choirs it is best to give additional blackboard exercises
in all keys, using numerals to denote the intervals.
The major and minor scales should be explained, and
exercises on them made the basis of a system of sight
reading. Useful hints on reading can be judiciously
combined with the practice of hymns, anthems, etc. Any
of the numerous manuals of sight-singing exercises are
useful in commencing elementary work with a new
choir.

Choir-rules should be reduced to a minimum and
strictly enforced. Some of the best choirs in the
country have no printed rules whatever, while others
of less repute indulge in elaborate codes, elegantly
framed. It does not take long for a neglected rule to
become a "dead letter."

In the discipline and management of choristers two
things are necessary : *will power* and a *correct knowledge
of the boy character.* Without the former, control is
impossible : without the latter, energy is wasted. That
obedience which proceeds from fear is better than none,
but that which springs from respect and personal regard is the highest acknowledgment of a choir-master's
influence. Frederick Helmore says, " Keep up by all
means a proper *esprit de corps ;* encourage good singers by occasional presents, but not of so great value
as to make them mercenary ; keep their minds bright

both in school and play-ground ; take them out for excursions when practicable ; let them see beautiful scenery, good pictures and statuary, in fact everything to refine and cultivate the taste, for every musical boy is an incipient artist. Find amusement for them on long winter evenings, in any little mechanical or useful employment for which they may show talent, and you will have a choir of bright-eyed, intelligent boys, who will sing to death any of your choirs of snubbed and neglected miserables."

The voices of boys skilfully trained, *resemble in quality the voices of women.* The chief difference is that women produce a more *mature* quality (the result of longer development and higher intelligence), while boys sing with more freshness, elasticity, and buoyancy. When voices are trained all alike by the correct method, they become homogeneous and blend together so that in chorus it is difficult for the ear to separate the voices.

In "meetings" of choirs trained badly and by different methods, the individual peculiarities of the different choirs combine to destroy *unity of timbre.*

Defects of impure voicing are modified and lessened by the resonant qualities of buildings. In a *large church*, with *tiled floor* and *lofty roof*, a harsh choir will sound tolerably well, excepting to the people in the front pews who are near the choristers.

Place the same choir in a *small, carpeted church,* and the vocal coarseness will stand boldly out in all its impurity. In accordance with an acoustic law governing timbre, the overtones and upper partials concerned in harshness indirectly affect the ear in buildings wanting resonance, while in buildings of great resonance, the fundamental tones are the ones chiefly reinforced, and the overtones and upper partials are lost to the ear. When acoustic resonance favors a choir, it affords no excuse for allowing the choristers to sing harshly. As before seen, training which permits such a result is physiologically wrong. Besides, resonance, while it helps to cover up the blemish of coarse singing, *equally enhances the beauty of pure singing.*

While a too frequent changing of services and anthems is undesirable, fresh music should be added constantly to the choir library. Music that is "sung out" or distasteful will always be rendered indifferently. Strong and vigorous compositions, on the other hand, inspire enthusiasm. A refined classic taste is easily engendered if standard music is used. Boys keenly appreciate the works of the great masters, and will often show undisguised contempt for weak and insipid compositions.

In connection with this it may be added that, choirs which are confined to the rendering of the music for morning and evening prayer, neglecting the music for the chief service of the Church, which is the Holy Eucharist, are necessarily cut off from the very fountain-head of ecclesiastical music. It cannot be expected, however, that music for the Holy Eucharist will ever receive its proper attention, until that highest Act of Worship is rendered as a service by itself.

Church music is of two kinds : Active and Meditative. Active or "Congregational" music is represented by hymns, chants, and the easier parts of the service, in which the people are expected vocally to join. Meditative music, consisting of anthems and the more elaborate portions of the service, although too difficult for the congregation to sing, nevertheless arouses higher forms of spiritual activity. Both kinds should be combined at every service.

Unless a choir is trained to depend chiefly upon itself, and not upon the accompaniment, numberless catastrophies are likely to occur. Processional hymns will be sung out of tune, a feeling of helplessness will pervade all piano passages, quiet organ accompaniment cannot be attempted without loss of pitch, and the many beautiful effects of unaccompanied singing will necessarily be lost.

Flattening proceeds, firstly, from bad methods of singing. Secondly, from dependence upon instrumental assistance. Thirdly, from certain conditions of the atmosphere (dampness, sultriness, etc.); and fourthly, from indolence and lack of enthusiasm in singers.

It cannot be too often impressed upon choristers that *piano* singing requires *strict mental attention*, without which there is sure to be *careless control of breath*, and consequent deterioration of tone. There is such a thing as *soft*, yet *energetic*, singing. *Piano* singing makes unusual demands upon the *mental faculties*, and this is the chief reason why it is so difficult to train boys to render soft passages *effectively*. The tendency to *drag* in singing softly is to be specially guarded against. Troutbeck, in his "Church Choir Training," observes : " Forcing the voice makes people sing sharp, and by inducing needless fatigue, at last makes them sing flat—in a word, destroys just intonation. The same loss of just intonation follows from a feeble, uncertain quality of tone. By a feeble tone is not at all meant a subdued or *piano* method of singing. Singing *piano* is generally not one of the first things learnt by a choir. It too often involves loss of pitch, and more often, loss of pace, as if *piano* and *lento* were interchangeable words."

In practising difficult passages, they should be taken *slowly* at first, and the tempo increased afterward. This is specially necessary in securing decisive attack, when the four parts enter, rapidly and at different places, in a given bar. Also in passages demanding flexibility.

A metronome should be kept in the rehearsal-room, both for reference and practice. By the aid of it choristers can be trained to rely upon themselves in counting, and to render difficult unaccompanied choruses with absolute accuracy of tempo.

Much discretion should be used in assigning solos, and care taken not to tax the voices too severely. Elaborate solos are usually beyond the reach of boys, and it is in the short solos and verse parts introduced between the movements of anthems that they are heard to the best advantage.

It has been seen (page 36) that the period of "change" in a boy's voice is marked by a temporary loss of control over the larynx, caused by uneven development of the cartilages and muscles. Mutation affects voices in various ways. Some boys change very gradually, the vocal bands and the parts affecting them developing slowly and evenly. In such cases the boy simply loses his top notes one by one, until his voice settles into tenor, baritone, or bass. Others lose their middle or lower notes first, and afterward the higher notes. There is no certainty about the matter, different voices changing in different ways. Although a skilful voice-trainer can at times so manage a boy's voice that he can sing all through mutation without injury, nevertheless the rule, "Stop singing when the change appears," should seldom, if ever, be disregarded.

Finally, it should be borne in mind by every choirmaster, that his position is not altogether identical with that of a teacher of singing.

There are further responsibilities connected with his work, which, if he be an earnest Churchman, he can scarcely fail to see. "The part which a chorister is called upon to take in an expressive and beautiful ritual, cannot fail to be well and impressively done, if its meaning and character be pointed out and understood; and a reverence of heart and gesture will surely follow, when the solemnity, and dignity, of the privilege he is allowed to exercise in the employment of the great gifts with which he is endowed by God, are impressed upon his mind." It should therefore be our constant endeavor to promote a feeling of thoughtfulness and reverence among the boys of the choir, that they may fulfil their duties not merely as *singers*, but as *devout children of the Church.*

CHAPTER IX.

SINCE the first issue of this work, in 1888, six editions have been exhausted, and several other treatises on the vocal training of boys have appeared.* Not only in ecclesiastical circles, but in schools and in other quarters, there has sprung up a growing interest in the subject.

The wholesome demand for information regarding boy voice-culture indicates, in no uncertain way, a steady progress toward a higher standard of excellence in the singing of choristers.

The previous chapters have given the views of eminent authorities on voice training, and have covered the more important points to be observed in teaching boys to sing. While little remains to be added, there are some questions which deserve further consideration.

The analogy between the voices of boys, of girls, and of women, touched upon in Chapter III., pages 35 and 36, and Chapter VIII., page 73, is a matter frequently lost sight of.

The remark of astonishment, " Why, he sings like a woman !" is by no means uncommon, after the performance of a capable boy soloist. Undoubtedly one reason why the rough vocal delivery of poorly trained

* Prominent among these are The Boy's Voice, by Curwen, published in 1891, and Choir-boy Training, by Martin, published in 1892.

choristers does not create more pronounced criticism among musical people is, that such singing is considered to be perfectly "natural." While the same kind of performance from women would not be tolerated, in boys it is condoned, and sometimes admired, on the supposition that it represents their special and privileged style of vocalization.

The following quotation is taken from a paper, written by the author at the request of the Choir Guild of the Diocese of Massachusetts, in 1894 :

"The larynges of boys and girls show no differences. They are anatomically alike. If, by way of experiment, we should train a boy and a girl from early childhood to use their voices gently, not only in singing, but also in conversation ; if we should develop from the first, purity of tone and ease of production, their singing voices would be precisely similar. If hidden behind a screen, and made to sing, after such a course of training, no living expert could tell one voice from the other. The girl's voice and the boy's being similar, what is the difference between the girl's and the woman's ? It is a difference in *maturity* more than in anything else. Anatomically, there are but slight laryngeal changes after pubescence. The girl, trained to avoid the thick register in childhood, rarely has any trouble with coarseness of tone when she becomes a woman.

Things which are equal to the same thing, are equal to each other. If the boy's voice is like the girl's, and the girl's like the woman's, the analogy between all three is far from obscure. It is well, then, to teach boy choristers to copy, as closely as possible, the *cultivated* voices of women."

On the other hand, it must not be forgotten that some women receive vocal instruction too late, and retain a voice production of marked roughness, exactly like that of ill-trained boys. This does not contravene what is said in the Preface, page 7, regarding the comparative purity of female voices. (See also foot-note, page 36.)

On page 60 it is stated that the thin register should be extended downward "*as far as possible.*"

Choir-masters, who are tardy converts to physiological methods, are inclined to hold out against this advice. They claim that the timbre of the thick register is necessary below the "break," in order to impart more brilliancy to the voice. A more fatal mistake cannot be made than that of strengthening the lower notes by the retention of more or less "thick" quality. The "break" should not be merely smoothed, modified, or lessened—it should be *eradicated.* This cannot be accomplished by any compromise system of training, which aims at securing the purity of the upper register, *and* the reedy timbre of the lower. When the break is not completely removed, boys will sing out of tune, both sharp and flat.

The directions of the standard authorities leave small margin for experiments on this point. They all state that when the break exists, there is danger of forcing the thick tones too high.

Now, is there any danger in carrying the thin register down *too low?* Certainly not. This is best answered by Madame Seiler, on page 66 of "The Voice in Singing :"

"We may not preserve the action of a lower series for the tones of a higher. On the other hand, the vocal organs show no straining when the action of a higher series of tones is kept for a lower." The distinguished authorities, Browne and Behnke, in enjoining the exclusive use of the thin register above E on the first line of treble stave, practically deny the thick register to sopranos, as whole services, and scores of chants, hymns, and anthems, include comparatively few notes below the one named. Their exact directions are, " It will be particularly necessary to prevent boys from carrying their thick registers above 🎵."

It is a significant fact that they fail to speak of the "particular necessity" of using the thick register below that point.*

The lack of vocal strength, mentioned on page 47, as a temporary result of confining voices to the upper register is apt to cause lack of faith in the possibility of finally securing sufficient fulness of tone.

" Thin," as a technical expression, is one of real scientific value in describing a register ; yet it is an infelicitous one for some reasons. Voice trainers, who are fond of noisy singing, are tempted to hide the technical, and emphasize the colloquial, meaning of the term. As the use of the thin register literally produces, at first, thin (weak) tone, the play upon the word is unfortunate. But, on the other hand, " thick " admirably expresses the disagreeable tone quality of the lower register.

There are other reasons, besides lack of faithful, patient teaching, which go far toward explaining the rarity of artistically trained choirs. The ability to distinguish between the nicer gradations of timbre varies greatly in different individuals.

* The Child's Voice, page 38.

We meet here another analogy, that between visual and aural defects.   Many people of keen eyesight are totally blind to certain variations of color ; so, also, are some persons of musical sensibilities deaf to the finer degrees of *tone color*.   Thus we find that what passes as pure quality with one, will offend the ear of a second, whose accurate perception of timbre will be called in question by a *third*.

Mr. A. may feel proud of the beautifully smooth singing of his boys, while Mr. B. may detect a mixture of coarseness in their work, which will deprive him of all pleasure in listening to them.

In regard to the question of boy altos, the author's experience bears out everything that has been said in Chapter VI.   Either the adult male alto should be well trained to his work, or boys should carry the pure quality through the alto compass.   In cases where choir-masters endeavor to confine the trebles to the thin register, allowing the altos to use thick tone, one of two results must follow : Either the alto part sounds unbearably coarse through contrast with the treble, or (what is more probable) the trebles fail to maintain sweetness of timbre on low notes, through unconscious imitation of the altos.   " Breaks " then begin to make their appearance, with their concomitant, out-of-tune singing.

If boys must sing alto, let them be treated rather as second trebles singing the alto part.   It is the best way to secure delicate tone quality.

While unison services are to be recommended as an occasional change from harmonized settings, much unison singing is detrimental to the maintenance of good quality.

Choristers are prone to copy the roughness of timbre from the basses, and even the basses themselves will develop bad delivery when a great deal of unison music is used. It gives the voices too much work between ♩ and ♩. This is one reason why Gregorian tones are bad for boys' voices. The truth of the matter is, Gregorian music was not originally intended for sopranos—either boys or women.

"The ponderous thunder of the plainsong was never produced by the child's treble. If we must revive that sort of thing now, we shall succeed better with massive choirs of men. There is nothing that will tear a boy's voice to pieces quicker than Gregorian chanting. It leads to *fortissimo singing, coarseness,* and *voice fatigue.*" *

The results derived from correct training are many, but the most important may be summed up as follows:

1. Beautiful timbre—a limpid, fluid quality, which causes a peculiar blending effect, making many voices sound as one.

2. Extension of compass, bringing high notes within very easy reach.

3. The total absence of the "break."

4. Singing "a cappella" without deviation from pitch.

5. Ability to sing for a long time without fatigue—the voices at the end of a three-hour service being as fresh as at the beginning.

6. Longevity of the treble voice—the signs of mutation appearing in many cases after the age of seventeen.

* Author.

The introduction of vested females into church choirs has recently been attempted, both in England and America. As a bold innovation, violating ecclesiastical tradition, it has met with the denunciation it deserves. Where choir-boys cannot be obtained, it is advisable to employ females ; but they should not occupy seats in the chancel, and they should not be robed in the ecclesiastical vestments of men and boys.

It is a great mistake to suppose that the best choirs are necessarily those in which women sing. The most celebrated choirs in the world are those of England and Russia, and they are composed exclusively of boys and men. The music performed by the Russian choirs is of the most difficult character. It is *strictly unaccompanied*, and, from the voice trainers' stand-point, *exacting in the highest degree.*

The uncultivated voice of the woman is not as rough as the raw boy voice, and it undergoes no change of "mutation." Nevertheless, there are disadvantages to be met with in teaching women to sing, not the least of which is the difficulty they often experience in taking high notes. The boy voice is *young* and *plastic*, and yields readily to treatment. The adult female frequently possesses vocal defects which should have been removed in youth, and which have become *fixed* and incurable.

The author has often noticed in the singing of choral societies a certain lack of elasticity in the voices, on notes above . This peculiarity has been mentioned by Curwen. On page 32 of "The Boy's Voice" he says, "Boys attack high notes with greater ease than women." Martin, on page 10 of his book on "Choir-boy Training," says, "Those who have had much to do with training the voices of women and boys, find by experience that the upper notes of the voice in women

are difficult to get, and when obtained, are neither so powerful nor so tuneful as the same notes in boys' voices."

CURRENT METHODS

OF

TRAINING BOYS' VOICES

A PAPER WRITTEN FOR THE

MASSACHUSETTS CHOIR GUILD

BY

G. EDWARD STUBBS, M.A., MUS.DOC.

*Organist of St. Agnes' Chapel, Trinity Parish ; Instructor in Church
Music in the General Theological Seminary, New York*

THE H. W. GRAY CO.

SOLE AGENTS FOR

NOVELLO & CO., Ltd.

21 EAST 17TH STREET, NEW YORK

PREFATORY NOTE.

In compliance with a request to write a paper on the "Boy Voice," for the Massachusetts Choir Guild, the leading difficulty encountered in teaching boys to sing has been kept steadily in view—*i.e.*, the blending of the registers so as to eliminate *entirely* the acquired timbre of the lower notes of the average untrained voice. No attempt has been made to say anything "new"—indeed there is little new to say. The art of training the boy voice was brought to the very highest perfection by the Italians, years and years ago. The vocal theories lately promulgated and proved by scientists, were anticipated by them in practice resulting from that musical acumen which seems to have been a National characteristic. In a previous publication * the writer has spoken of the general details of choir training ; nevertheless it cannot be too often asserted that the thick register of the boy voice is NOT what Nature designed for singing. If this short essay contributes even in a limited degree to the dissemination of that vital truth, it may not fail to serve a useful purpose.

G. E. S.

St. Agnes' Chapel, Trinity Parish, New York,
January, 1894.

* "Practical Hints on the Training of Choir Boys." Novello, Ewer and Co., London and New York.

PREFACE TO THE SECOND EDITION.

THE first edition of this essay provoked considerable discussion among choir-masters, and, curiously enough, encountered the criticism that it presented untenable theories, which clashed with those set forth in the writer's " Practical Hints on the Training of Choir Boys." There is, of course, no disagreement between the two publications. The similarity between the voices of *boys*, *girls*, and *women*, correctly trained, is affirmed by scientists, and by the best teachers of singing. For reasons which will appear,* the views herein taken on this particular point are not, and perhaps never will be, held by the great majority of choir-masters. Nevertheless they are founded upon physiological truth, are maintained by the highest authorities, and are unassailable.

G. E. S.

ST. AGNES' CHAPEL, TRINITY PARISH, NEW YORK,
January, 1898.

* Page 99, lines 27–28.

CURRENT METHODS

OF

TRAINING BOYS' VOICES.

THE prevailing methods pursued in the cultivation of boys' voices may be traced to three sources of training —Public Schools, Sunday Schools, and Church Choirs. There is seldom any provision made in select schools for voice culture ; not one boy in a thousand takes private lessons from a singing master, and there are in this country few, if any, choral classes organized solely for children. The systems of vocal training which are at all far-reaching, and which exert a widespread effect upon boys' voices, emanate from the sources mentioned.

Of boys under regular vocal instruction, probably ninety - nine per cent. receive it from schools and choirs ; and of these a percentage nearly as high—so high I dislike to estimate it by figures—practise singing under a peculiarly crude method, so extensively used that it may be considered *universal.*

Should, for the sake of experiment, a chorus of boys' voices, selected at random from these three sources— say a thousand from each—be subjected to critical vocal examination, a large majority of the three thousand

voices would show unmistakable evidence of having
been trained under a distinctive method of voice production—that which extends and develops the thick
register—a system condemned by *all* standard vocal
authorities as based upon a false physiological foun-
dation.

This may seem a sweeping and exaggerated statement, yet it is a perfectly true one, and in searching
for an explanation of it we need not look very far.
The cultivation of children's voices upon sound physiological principles, represents a neglected branch of
education. Vocal instruction, in its public school sense,
really means practice in sight reading. The pupils are
taught notation, and are trained to read at sight, exercises written on the blackboard. They are free to
follow their own inclinations as to voice production.
Culture of the voice therefore forms an insufficient
part of public school education. I am aware that in
some schools effort is made to prevent shouting and
coarseness of singing, but the exceptions are too few
to invalidate the general statement I have made.

Vocal instruction, taken in its Sunday-school sense,
means the singing of melodies from memory. Hymns,
carols, etc., etc., are practised over and over again,
until they are learnt by ear. Culture of the voice,
therefore, forms an insufficient part of the musical
training given in Sunday-schools.

In choirs a somewhat better state of things exists,
yet vocal instruction, in its church choir sense, too
often resembles that found in the schools. In many
choirs the boys learn to sing chiefly from memory. In
some, they are taught notation and sight reading. In
comparatively few is voice *culture* made a special feat-

ure of choir work, and carried to a high degree of perfection. It must be admitted, therefore, that culture
of the voice forms an insufficient part of the musical
instruction given to choirs.

All this accounts for the low condition of voice-
training under which the majority of boys unfortu-
nately fall. Whether correct methods will ever be successfully, and extensively, introduced in public schools
and Sunday-schools, is a question too difficult to solve.
With regard to church-choirs the outlook is brighter.
The rapidly increasing number of male-choirs has cre-
ated a demand for skilful voice trainers, and choir-
masters are now giving greater attention to the study
of vocal culture than formerly, when women (whose
voices are comparatively free from *acquired* defects)
were employed as choristers.

I have stated that an enormously high percentage
of boys are trained to sing by false and pernicious
methods, based upon the development and extension
of the thick register. It would be perhaps unnecessary, and out of place, here to enter into the scientific
details of vocal physiology. I assume that choir-trainers, who are alive to the needs of the times, are more
or less familiar with the current literature on the Boy
Voice, with the generally accepted laws of voice-culture, and their special bearing upon children's voices.
It is, however, one thing to know a theory by rote, and
quite a different thing to know it from actual practice
and experience. While a great many choir-masters
may be acquainted with the law forbidding the extension of the thick register, it is unquestionably true that
few *obey* it. There seems to be a decided reluctance to
being bound down to vocal precepts. It is not an un-

common thing to hear the merits of the "chest tone system," and the "head tone system," discussed as if it were purely a matter of taste which should be employed.

Boys, if left to themselves, use the thick register almost exclusively in singing, and this leads to the well-nigh incurable belief that it is perfectly right for them to do so, and that "natural" tendencies should not be interfered with. Even prominent choir-masters are sometimes carried away with this idea. I have been told by some of the most distinguished organists in England that they did not believe in spending much time on the voice-culture of their boys, or in changing their usual habits of singing. "Do not impose too much restraint. Give them a few scales to strengthen their voices, and they will come out all right," is a doctrine I have heard expounded in more than one English rehearsal-room. And so, among choir-trainers in a country supposed to be pre-eminently famous for the pure singing of choristers, this universal method of mis-training a boy's voice abounds.

The attention of English choir-masters was called to this fact not very long ago by an able lecture given by Dr. Bates, organist of Norwich Cathedral. He took the ground that the cultivation of boys' voices was shamefully neglected ; and in referring to a supposed scarcity of good voices among English boys, he unhesitatingly laid the blame where it belonged—upon the shoulders of those responsible for that neglect. Instead of to a dearth of fine voices, he pointed to a lack of experienced trainers, and maintained that excellent voices were constantly being ruined by wrong methods of teaching.

At the root of the matter lies the forcing of the lower register and its upward extension. Until the fallacy of this crude and injurious system of developing the voice is more thoroughly understood, voice-culture must remain at a standstill in our schools and choirs.

There should be a wider recognition of the need of more expert voice-training. If head-masters, and their assistants, would but give proper attention to the subject, they would be able to prevent, in great measure, the wretched singing so common in schools. Among church organists, who are responsible for the direction of the choral service, there is a tendency to belittle the importance of choir-training. As Sir Joseph Barnby justly says, "everything runs to organ technique." Ability to play well is certainly an indispensable part of the choir-master's education—but that should not absorb every energy. Taking for granted the special qualifications of the disciplinarian, progress in training boys' voices requires further : *First.*—Vocal knowledge. *Second.*—A keen, discriminating EAR. *Third.*—Patience to work on right principles for slow results. The established laws of voice-culture must first be MASTERED, especially those referring to the management of the registers. The EAR is then called into use, to DETECT variations of timbre, whether well-marked or slight. Patience is then demanded, to slowly build the voice upon legitimate methods. Lack of knowledge, lack of ear, lack of patience—any of the three is sufficient to prevent success.

Among sundry communications which I have received from time to time from choir-masters, I call to mind several from well-meaning, industrious, and enthusiastic men, who were hard at work ill-treating the voices of their choristers without knowing it. One of these came from a voice-trainer in Northern New York, who had achieved such a measure of success * with his choir that it was regarded all over that part of the State as the best organized, and best managed, to be found anywhere. I was appealed to for a list of services and anthems written with a low soprano part, "going no higher than E on the fourth space," with which to replenish an exhausted *répertoire* of similar compositions. The letter gave a glowing history of the choir and its work, but deplored the fact that *the climate of Northern New York* prevented the boys from singing higher than the aforesaid E.

Soon after this letter came a longer one from a choirmaster of Liverpool, England, asking if it were not permissible for his boys to intone the Creed and various other parts of the service in the thick register, and declaring that it was an utter impossibility to prevent their doing so. The writer was a man of wide experience, and had trained boy voices for *more than twenty years.*

The following I quote from an English authority :

"In spite of all that can be written on the subject of voice-training, the art is one most difficult to communicate. Some teachers succeed ; others fail. A remarkable instance of this came under my notice

---

* The average musical ear demands first *rhythm ;* then *melody ; last of all, tone quality.* Impure voicing sometimes escapes condemnation when "things go together," and with sufficient *éclat.* "Popular" success, and *artistic* success, are two widely different things.

lately. The head-master of a school asked me to pay his boys a visit, in order to discover, if possible, the reason of the great falling off in their singing. His previous singing teacher had brought the boys to a high pitch of excellence. When he left, the singing was placed under the charge of an under-master, who had for a year or more heard all the singing lessons given by his predecessor, *who used the same voice exercises, with the same boys, in the same room.* Surely one would have thought the results must be the same. But the singing had deteriorated ; flattening, and a lifeless manner had overcome the boys. The causes, so far as I could discover, were, first, that the new teacher wanted the magnetic, enthusiastic way of the old ; and, second, that he had not so quick an ear for change of register, and allowed the lower mechanism of the voice to be forced up higher than its proper limits."

Among similar instances, I remember a prominent choir which had been skilfully trained to use correct voice production, and which was handed over to a new choir-master. Inside of a month he completely undid all that had been accomplished, and taught the choristers to use the wrong method. The opportunity of continuing the former system of training was thrown away and the singing soon degenerated.

Any number of such illustrations could be given, but these are sufficient to show briefly the importance of correct knowledge and a good ear. Without both, a *false start* is inevitably made, and as inevitably *continued.*

The patience necessary to produce fulness and strength, throughout the thin register, is a third factor of success, not easily overestimated. The *growth* of the voice—the production of *power*—is a slow process, in many cases slow enough to severely shake the confidence of those who have not learned to wait for Nature to take her course. Lack of patience is ofttimes associated with lack of *faith in the results to be attained by confining voices to the proper register.* That the thin register is capable of immense development, that the greatest choirs in the world use it exclusively, with telling effect—these are facts not fully grasped by the majority of choir-masters. Great faith is wanted in building the voice up from the tiny thread of tone first heard at the commencement of correct training, especially in those cases where previous misuse of voice has led to almost total obliteration of the upper register. The difficulty and delay experienced in strengthening the lower part of the voice may, and undoubtedly does, lead in some cases to the abandonment of proper methods, even when they are known.*

Thus it happens that from want of knowledge, ear, or patience, choirs are not infrequently taught to use thick tone exclusively, or else to jump about from one register to the other, according to the exigencies of the occasion.

Space does not here admit of many observations on choir-training. I wish in this brief paper to simply emphasize the importance of downward extension of

* A very common objection to choirs trained to downward extension of the thin register is that they lack "verve," are ineffective, and show a decided want of brilliancy, power, and breadth of tone. Weakness and insufficiency of tone are remediable defects; they exist, to be sure, but not in the best choirs. Both pianissimo and fortissimo passages receive thoroughly adequate interpretation in choirs where there is not the slightest vestige of thick tone. Among many notable illustrations may be cited the choir of St. Paul's Cathedral, London; the choirs of Trinity College, Oxford, Magdalen College, Oxford, etc., etc.

the thin register, whereby not only is pure tone quality obtained, but what is of greater importance, *correct
mechanism* of the vocal organs is secured. This should
take precedence in all details of voice-teaching. Everything else should be secondary to it. Resonance,
flexibility, attack, articulation, phrasing, etc., etc.—all
these should receive attention AFTER the right mechanism is taught. Notwithstanding the recent publication, both here and abroad, of treatises on the Boy
Voice,* this one cardinal principle remains a sticking-
point with many choir-masters. The habitual use of
the thin register throughout the entire vocal compass
is looked upon by not a few voice-trainers as a "fad,"
encouraged and followed only by a few specialists.
*That it embodies the old Italian method, practised for ages
and ages by the choir-masters of Italy, and later introduced
into England, and still later defended in extenso by modern
scientists, is a fact either unknown or ignored.*
I have heard some curious questions raised regarding the exclusive use of the thin register—whether it
was not unnatural to practise it ; whether it did not
develop serious weakness of tone ; whether it did not
damage the future man's voice ; whether it was first
"invented" and used by X. Y. Z., a Philadelphia choir-
master, or by Z. Y. X., a New York choir-master ;
whether it did not lead to a species of "falsetto" singing, etc., etc., etc., *ad infinitum.* So strong is the impression that the boy's rough and rasping low register is

* "Practical Hints on the Training of Choir Boys," by G. Edward
Stubbs. Novello, Ewer and Co., 1888.
"The Boys' Voice," by J. S. Curwen. Curwen and Sons, 1891.
"Choir Boy Training," by Sir G. C. Martin. Novello, Ewer and
Co., 1892.

the one Nature meant him to sing with, it has become a
matter of the gravest difficulty to make any SUCCESS-
FUL crusade against that popular and persistent con-
viction. If we probe this subject to the bottom, we
shall find that much of the mischief proceeds from a
radical misconception as to *what the boy voice really is.*
From the voice-trainer's standpoint, IT IS THE WOMAN'S
VOICE. It would be a blessing if the term "boy voice"
could be abolished entirely. It insensibly tends to fos-
ter the idea that Nature fully *intended* the boy to have
a singing voice perfectly unique in itself, and different from any other kind ; one endowed with a marked
and powerful reedy timbre, which should be looked
upon as its legitimate characteristic, and which should
rightfully entitle it to a distinctive and special name.
Small wonder that choristers skilfully trained are ac-
cused of singing "falsetto" ! !

The larynges of boys and girls show no differences.
They are anatomically alike. If, by way of experiment, we should train a boy and a girl from early
childhood to use their voices gently, not only in singing, but also in conversation ; if we should develop,
from the first, purity of tone and ease of voice production, their singing voices would be *precisely similar.* If
hidden behind a screen, and asked to sing, after such
a course of training, *no living expert could at first trial
tell one voice from the other.* Distinction could only result from slight individual characteristics, which might
be apparent to those intimately acquainted with the
voices, and which might not. The same experiment
would hold good if from their childhood they should
be taught to abuse the lower register. Both would sing
the same way, and again if concealed from view, *no*

one would be able to distinguish between the voices. That girls are apt to use the thin register to a considerable extent, is largely due to their quiet dispositions, and to the fact that they do not partake in rough and bois- terous games. And yet in schools they are sometimes heard to produce almost as disagreeable a quality of tone as boys. In either sex the coarseness of the lower register may be ACQUIRED by bad habits of voice use, or SUPPRESSED entirely by gentle speaking and singing.

The girl's voice and the boy's being similar, what is the difference between the girl's and the woman's? It is a difference in maturity * more than in anything else. Anatomically, there are but slight laryngeal changes after pubescence. The girl trained to avoid the thick register in childhood, rarely has any trouble with coarseness of tone when she becomes a *woman.* Her voice presents one smooth and even compass throughout. If, on the other hand, the early training has been bad, later in life her voice must receive the treatment it should have had. *The woman's voice, in short, is trained like a girl's, as far as blending of registers is concerned.* There must be no "break," and no coarseness of tone.

Things which are equal to the same thing are equal to each other. If the boy's voice is like the girl's, if the girl's is like the woman's, the analogy between all three is far from obscure. I think not enough has been made of this point in treatises on the boy voice. *That surprise should be so generally expressed when boys sing like women, is most unfortunate.* The chief feat- ure of the well-trained female voice is that it has no

* For a full investigation of this interesting subject see "Voice, Song, and Speech," by Browne and Behnke.

break ; so also is that the chief feature in the case of the trained boy. In both the registers are so far blended that it is impossible to detect any line of demarcation between them. The right mechanism is used ; there is neither straining after high notes, nor coarseness on low ones. The boy's voice and the woman's, then, are fundamentally one and the same thing, and are to be trained virtually on the same lines.

That it is a matter of no little difficulty to smooth the voices of boys, cannot be denied. And yet how readily does the voice yield to treatment when once under control ! Its capabilities are, partly from ignorance and partly from prejudice, greatly underestimated. Like a piece of soft clay, the boy's voice is *plastic*. It is capable of marvellous development ; it shows in course of time singular purity, and it exceeds in range the *adult female* * voice.

It cannot be too often repeated that the rasping timbre of the boy's lower register is an ACQUIRED rather than a NATURAL characteristic. Women are free from it simply because their methods of life lead to a subdued and refined voice production. Should they habitually yell and scream in the streets, play baseball, football, and similar out-door sports, *as boys play them*, they would *vocally* become converted into *boys* in very short order.

---

* Boys' voices are more elastic and extensible than women's. This is well known to those who have had experience with both. It is undoubtedly owing to a more pliant condition of the vocal organs in childhood and youth. The same truth of course applies to girls' voices. I believe Dr. Martin, of St. Paul's Cathedral, is one of the few who have called attention to the fact that women are harder to train on high notes than boys.

It is well, then, to teach choristers to copy as closely as possible the cultivated voices of women. They should hear the best concerts, and more particularly the singing of oratorio societies, as often as opportunity presents, and they should be encouraged in every way to imitate the tonal effects obtained from female voices.

A word or two in conclusion, with regard to a matter which has an important bearing upon the culture of boys' voices. We are informed from time to time by the church press, and the clergy, that the advancement of our church music demands a more general return to the ancient plain song, and "unison" singing. Even if I propose to consider the question on the ground of ecclesiastical antiquity and propriety, I could not shake off a strong predilection for the views of Macfarren, Smart, S. S. Wesley, Jebb, and others. But what is more to the point here is the unquestionable damage wrought by making boys sing music written for the monks of the Middle Ages. The ponderous "thunder of the plain song" was never produced by the child's treble. If we must revive that sort of thing now, we shall succeed better with massive choirs of MEN.* There is hardly anything that will tear a boy's voice to pieces quicker than Gregorian chanting. *It leads to fortissimo singing, coarseness, and voice fatigue.* Both unison and Gregorian music, occasionally employed by way of contrast, is harmless

* Among examples of good Gregorian choirs in this country should be mentioned that of the Chapel of the Good Shepherd, General Theological Seminary, New York. During "term time" service is sung twice daily, all the men in the Seminary (about one hundred and thirty) taking par*

and even effective ; but the *constant* exercise of the
boy's voice upon music written low enough to tempt
him to use the wrong register, is pernicious in the
highest degree.   As women are often required to sing
Gregorian music, the question may be asked, " if they
stand the strain, why not boys ?   If the voices are alike,
why can't they be put to like work ? "   Women suffer
less from such singing, not only because their voices
are more matured by growth and are stronger, but
also because from long-continued use of the thin register they are less liable to "break."   Yet I doubt not
that their voices are often roughened by plain song
when extensively sung.   I have seen many choirs in
England and America absolutely ruined (as far as delicate tone quality goes) by excessive " unison " work.
Purity of tone, the right mechanism of voice—both
are with difficulty preserved where boy sopranos are
persistently kept upon unison services and Gregorian
chanting.*

Anything and everything that will discourage our
boy choristers from braying in the thick register,
should be most rigidly adopted in their training.

* While it is not absolutely impossible to train boy trebles on
" Gregorians " without injury, it is nearly so.   The two most famous Gregorian choirs (employing boy sopranos) in America are
those of St. Patrick's Cathedral, Fifth Avenue, and St. Paul's Church,
Ninth Avenue, New York.   Both choirs are of great size.   The
Cathedral boys sing at vespers on Sunday afternoons.   The St.
Paul's boys sing both morning and afternoon, and ALL of their music
is plain song, including the Mass.   Choir-masters desiring to investigate the effect of plain song on the boy voice, are recommended to
study these two choirs, and to draw their own conclusions.   As both
churches are very large and resonant, it is necessary to go close to
the singers to form any correct opinion of the voice quality.

They should be taught to avoid coarseness of singing as they would poison, and to learn the fullest meaning of that all-important precept, " he sings best who sings with least effort." In this way can we approach that old Italian art, which placed quality of tone above all else, and which by the most gentle and patient treatment, developed voices with a skill which may well seem unaccountable to us in this hasty age.

END